Rock Classics

# Kate Bush
# The Dreaming

Peter Kearns



SONICBOND PUBLISHING
sonicbondpublishing.com

Sonicbond Publishing Limited
www.sonicbondpublishing.co.uk
Email: info@sonicbondpublishing.co.uk

First Published in the United Kingdom 2024
First Published in the United States 2024

British Library Cataloguing in Publication Data:
A Catalogue record for this book is available from the British Library



ISBN 978-1-78952-341-6



Typeset in ITC Garamond Std & ITC Avant Garde Gothic
Printed and bound in England

Graphic design and typesetting: Full Moon Media

**Follow us on social media:**
Twitter: https://twitter.com/SonicbondP
Instagram: www.instagram.com/sonicbondpublishing_/
Facebook: www.facebook.com/SonicbondPublishing/

Linktree QR code:

# Kate Bush
# The Dreaming

## Contents

## Acknowledgements

Many thanks to Stephen Lambe
and the team at Sonicbond Publishing.

Rock Classics

Kate Bush

# The Dreaming

Peter Kearns

SONICBOND PUBLISHING
sonicbondpublishing.com

## Introduction: Strange Phenomena

In the twilight of an October evening in 1981, Kate Bush and bassist Del Palmer pulled up at the ruins of Urquhart Castle on the west side of Loch Ness in the Scottish Highlands. The trees surrounding the fifth-century fort were a multi-coloured array against the soundtrack of the rough, crashing waters beyond. A bit of casual monster hunting was relaxation after the wearying sessions for the partially complete and as-yet-untitled album that was to become *The Dreaming.* Shame about the water conditions, though, as Nessie was well-known to appear only when the Loch was dead still, and indeed, became the subject of yet another famous photograph purported to be of the monster that someone else took just one week later.

Kate has described the London of that period as having an 'air of doom'; thus, the need to get away. Exhausting recording sessions were one thing, but there was also the political climate – which was one of recession – dominated by the Brixton riots the prior April, proliferating into those in Handsworth (Birmingham), Chapeltown (Leeds) and Toxteth (Liverpool) in July.

Bush and Palmer made a break for it on a whim, heading north initially on the sleeper, and now here they were at Urquhart – temporary tourists, reading the sign telling of a phantom battle that once supposedly took place near where they stood. Heading back to the car, they were about to leave when Kate noticed three huge orange lights in the sky descending diagonally, then lining up horizontally and just sitting there, suspended. Trying to get closer, they drove around a bend, only to lose sight of the lights. Reappearing a few minutes later, there were now only two lights, and soon, they, too, were gone for good. The trip's most exhilarating event was over, but the intrepid duo did apparently indulge in some form of mountain climbing before making a beeline for the gaping hole of unfinished *Dreaming* that awaited them in London.

Ironically, mountain climbing was also one hobby of a man who, half a century before, had lived in a house just five miles down the road south but on the other side of Loch Ness. That man was announced to be the world's most wicked one – occultist Aleister Crowley – and the house was Boleskine House (owned by Led Zeppelin's Jimmy Page at the time of Bush's visit to Loch Ness). Some believe that Crowley performed some dark ceremony at Boleskine that unleashed forces manifesting as UFOs; they made their presence known around the time of his 1947 death. It's just *too* convenient to not refer to such an unbelievable tale here, considering Kate's proximity to Boleskine upon her UFO sighting, not to mention her lyrical propensity for references to strange phenomena. Further to this, UFO sightings in the area have been explained away as the mere manifestation of what's been called an *earthlight* phenomenon caused by the geological activity of the Great Glen Fault. But *that's* no fun, *is it?* Certainly, Kate paid this piffle no attention if you believe the rumour that, for a number of years afterwards, she officially endorsed a West Country UFO group, if only in spirit due to the requirement to prioritise more pressing affairs. Should you need further evidence of a (perhaps somewhat tenuous) Bush/Crowley connection, I refer you to Kate's 2011 single 'Wild Man', which refers to the Kangchenjunga Demon, more widely known as the Abominable Snowman or the Yeti. It just so happens that prior to Brown and Band's successful 1955 Kangchenjunga ascent, Aleister Crowley had come the closest, attempting an ascent in 1905, until four of his team were killed in an avalanche at 25,000 ft. Crowley then abandoned the attempt and retreated. After that, I have nothing re a Bush/Crowley connection, unless you consider the myth that Crowley and escapologist Harry Houdini (subject of the song 'Houdini' from *The Dreaming*) worked in collusion for British intelligence during World War I.

As unbelievable as some of the above surely is, it *is* appropriate, as Kate Bush's music is a cauldron of often seemingly unbelievable esoterica and ideas from the likes of psychoanalyst Wilhelm Reich and philosopher (and dancer, ironically enough) George Gurdjieff. Bush's work has been referred to as art rock and even progressive rock. But though the subject matter of prog rock was almost always fictional (certainly the early stuff), Bush's early lyrics more often sat on a knife edge of disbelief or were so sincerely delivered as to be – if not convincing, then at least – acceptable. Saying that, when it came to matters of the otherworldly, it wasn't easy to tell if she was a curious onlooker or a preaching zealot, as she so cooly managed to slip these ideas into the late 1970s mainstream. Her songs made reference to such harmless pop-culture iconography as serenading saxophones and Hammer films, while exhorting the public in, holding them there in the unsettling leer of bulging, mascaraed eyes, telling us things like, 'It could be just lust, but it will be fun', and slipping-in the more-intense, 'No more under the quilt to keep you warm/Your sister I was born', while we were still digesting the 'lust' bit. But you couldn't look away. Combine that with the cavorting in the 'Wuthering Heights' video, filmed on Salisbury Plain during Halloween week 1977, and you *could* have a link in a cultural through-line running perhaps from Mumau's silent 1922 film *Nosferatu,* to the 1971 Ken Russell movie *The Devils*, to the music of Black Sabbath and Led Zeppelin, to the groundbreaking horror flick *The Exorcist,* right through to the massively reverberating 1999 endgame door slam that was Stanley Kubrick's *Eyes Wide Shut.* Since then, the public's willingness to accept such ideas as entertainment has perhaps waned despite a thousand noble Scandinavian black-metal bands attempting to quell the quelling. *Or,* 'Wuthering Heights' and its siblings could've all just been a pleasant young lady with a high voice, singing relatively high-concept lyrics over harmonically complex compositions that happened to become hits. I think Kate might subscribe to that last notion and probably describe it more eloquently.

However, that whole idea doesn't change the fact that the woman and her music did – and still do – captivate. None were more captivated than the group of German EMI representatives, cameramen and onlookers present in Munich in the summer of 1980 for the dress rehearsal of mimed 'Babooshka' and 'Army

Dreamers' performances, which were to be filmed in front of a live audience later that day for the German television show *RockPop*. The seven minutes of performance encapsulated Bush's undeniable professionalism, versatility and seemingly effortless ability to enthral. Again, impossible to look away, especially during 'Babooshka', when, clad in a bright red pantsuit, the Kent lass theatrically relayed her story based on an English (not Russian) folk tale, all while clasping and manhandling a double bass that all-but dwarfed her despite her obvious control over the instrument, ending in her strangling its neck (a clear extension of the story, though not referred to in the lyric). In fact, her entire facial characterisation in the performance was a virtual emotional displacement of the story's seemingly innocent wife, who now obviously had nothing but evil on her mind – revealed immediately by the circumspect glare that a conspiracy theorist might describe as lizard-like (no freeze-framing required).

Soon after, Kate reappeared on the *RockPop* stage as virtually unrecognisable, dressed as a wartime laundress replete with kerchief and unkempt clothing, for her choreographed rendition of the coming single 'Army Dreamers'. But now, the evil was replaced with humour, the chorus' steps seemingly taking cues from Morris dancing and the *Monty Python's Flying Circus* fish-slapping sketch. In fact, one of the accompanying male dancers even looked *remarkably* like Python member Eric Idle. Interestingly, the track played for longer to include the actual ending not heard on the record.

These performances were living proof of Bush's skill as an entertainer and her ability to hold an audience in the palm of her hand and keep them there, and we haven't even really touched on anything musical yet. Bush is/was one of the last in a long lineage of theatre and music-hall tradition – and to think she'd been nervous about the latter performance all *day*. But as far as she was concerned, it wasn't about her; nothing she's ever done *has* been, other than her overriding conviction to be true to herself within the overarching values. One of those values has always been politeness – approaching the waiting journalists after the day's rehearsal, she refused to talk yet, saying, 'Oh god, I've got to go and have a shower. I feel all sort of ... you know'.

Mere weeks later, the *Never For Ever* album was just commencing its successful shelf life on the coattails of the global success of its two prior singles: 'Breathing' and 'Babooshka'. *The Dreaming* was, in effect, conceived that very week thanks to the unexpected and perhaps unlikely inspiration of – of all things – a Stevie Wonder concert. Kate and Del attended one three-hour-long Wonder show of his six September nights at Wembley Arena, meeting him backstage afterwards. Kate was a big Wonder fan, also having a taste for Steely Dan, Frank Zappa, Captain Beefheart and Devo, while her music remained impressively absent of those influences on the surface. Having said that, *The Dreaming* could be considered to contain some element of smooth foundation (orchestral, jazz and folk landmarks) beneath layers of angular harmony and sometimes unstable hysteria. That sure sounds like a blueprint for those four acts to me.

The Stevie Wonder concert seemed to cure Kate of the writer's block she'd been suffering, as she effortlessly wrote what was to become the album's opening track 'Sat In Your Lap' the following day. The lyric concerned the unreliable nature of knowledge and creativity itself, though – ironically – new songs continued to appear. But not before she purchased a large Victorian home on Court Road, Eltham, encircled by trees, privately situated back from the road. (The property was later to be named Wuthering Heights). There, she installed an eight-track demo studio, including a piano, a Yamaha CS-80 synthesizer and the new LinnDrum machine. Technology was becoming increasingly important for music creation at the time. Where Kate's older material was written at the piano before being worked and rehearsed with a band in the studio, the new songs began from the ground up with LinnDrum patterns and keyboard arrangements, the bulk of a lyric often appearing later in the process. Working fast, she came up with an idea and the musical bones of a song every night for several weeks. Not all were successful, but some of those at least yielded something that could be incorporated into one of the more fleshed-out songs.

The next consideration was whether to use a producer on the new record or not. Kate quickly dispatched the idea of again working with *Never For Ever* co-producer Jon Kelly, feeling that the music 'needed some kind of shock'; being the primary decision maker seemed to be the way to achieve it. However, David Bowie producer Tony Visconti *was* considered, and it got as far as a meeting with him. Visconti had been a fan of Kate's *Lionheart* album (1979), and she admired Bowie's Visconti-produced *Lodger* (also 1979): its influence apparent on parts of *The Dreaming*, according to some. But in the end, Kate sweetly retreated from the idea, saying, 'I've decided to produce the album myself. But, Tony, if there was a producer I'd work with, it would be you'.

## Recording The Dreaming

Though Kate had co-produced *Never For Ever* with Jon Kelly and had assisted Andrew Powell with the production of *Lionheart,* the decision to finally self-produce proper came from working with Peter Gabriel in January 1980, singing on his songs 'Games Without Frontiers' and 'No Self Control' for his third eponymous album (known as *Melt*). His method of crafting compositions by beginning with a drum machine intrigued Kate and set her on the path to thinking she could pull a whole album together herself. She eased herself into the position by co-producing *Never For Ever* that year with Jon Kelly. Once it came time to record *The Dreaming,* all she had to do was get all the musicians and engineers on her side, and it would all be fine. After the fact, she told Mick Brown of *The Guardian:*

> I think the basic fear in everybody's head was, 'God, does she really know what she's doing?'. But the one thing you learn is to trust your own decisions. When everyone else is saying, 'No, that's dangerous', there is always a little voice in my head saying, 'Yeah, yeah, it's alright'. In the past, I've maybe gone with somebody else's opinion because I felt I should, and I've never really felt happy with the result. This time, I've gotten closest to what I set out to achieve because I had that control.

Impressed with the famous gated drum sound that engineer/producer Hugh Padgham had achieved at London's Townhouse studio on the above-mentioned Peter Gabriel album, Kate enlisted Padgham and Townhouse to commence recording proper on her new album in May 1981. But the pairing lasted only a few weeks, recording only basic rhythm tracks and guide vocals for 'Sat In Your Lap', 'Leave It Open' and 'Get Out Of My House', including – as they all do – something similar to the infamous gated drum sound. Padgham was fitting the work in around other pressing engagements – like the production of The Police's album *Ghost In The Machine*

– and he became frustrated with Bush's constant adding of musical layers and seeming inability to tell if something was actually sounding good sonically. But they *did* complete 'Sat In Your Lap', which Kate rush-released as a single in June 1981. Perhaps adventurous listening for some, the angular and intellectual song reached number 11 in the UK anyway.

In Padgham's absence, Townhouse engineer Nick Launay took over. It was basically just he and Kate (and whatever musicians they happened to be working with) in an open frame of mind to push the envelope and try anything. That summer was warm – but with work to do, much concentration was needed to avoid succumbing to the temptation of the outdoors. The cutting-edge Fairlight CMI digital sampler and audio workstation (used on *Never For Ever*) still had an allure and was employed on most of *The Dreaming*. First hiring one from Syco Systems, Kate realised she couldn't live without the technology, purchasing her own £12,000 beast before the album was complete.

Over two months, rhythm tracks were recorded for 'Houdini', 'All The Love', 'There Goes A Tenner', 'The Dreaming' and 'Suspended In Gaffa', with a core of musicians consisting of drummers Stuart Elliott (Steve Harley & Cockney Rebel, Al Stewart) and Preston Heyman (later with Terence Trent D'Arby), bassists Del Palmer, Jimmy Bain (ex Rainbow, John Cale, Wild Horses) and guitarists Ian Bairnson (Pilot, The Alan Parsons Project), Alan Murphy (later of Go West and Level 42) and Brian Bath (The KT Bush Band). But in the end, only three tracks on the album used their recorded guitar parts.

Kate recorded 20 demos, of which ten songs became the album. The sessions were long and sometimes arduous. But there were no pre-rehearsals for the players – Kate would sit down and play a new song, the musicians usually hearing it for the first time. Between them, they'd work out an arrangement on the spot – meaning, for the players, sometimes after much experimentation and wrangling in the hopes of deciphering the form and metric details of the eccentric pieces. Kate's way of explaining her wishes, more in terms of metaphor and preferred feeling, sometimes confounded the process, Launay later saying, 'I don't think she had any realisation of how complex songs like 'The Dreaming' were. To her, they were very simple'. As a result, Launay did many edits of the rhythm tracks, realising the best backing for a particular song from multiple performances. It sounds hi-tech, but it was very common and was the same thing The Beatles had done from the beginning when, in the early 1960s, their producer George Martin assembled the perfect backing tracks for songs like 'She Loves You' and 'I Want To Hold Your Hand' by editing different takes together.

Whatever it took, it was all in aid of achieving what was in Kate's imagination and to satisfy her wish for the music to be cinematic. Her fleshed-out demos contained the bulk of the moods and sounds. The demo was always referred to before commencing the recording of a new song and often again during the process to retain focus.

In the midst of all the activity came an offer for Kate to play the Wicked Witch in the children's TV show *Worzel Gummidge.* Though tempted, she had to turn it down. Besides, there were other issues to deal with. With the Townhouse having pre-bookings and Launay's requirement to remain there, his role in the album was now complete, and Kate had to move to another studio. (It's worth mentioning that Launay's next major project was the production of Australian band Midnight Oil's *10, 9, 8, 7, 6, 5, 4, 3, 2, 1* – a thrilling and now criminally underrated record, and quite possibly Launay's greatest accomplishment. It is well worth it for the glorious (and unlikely) opener 'Outside World' alone, the backing track of which coincidentally but understandably bears an experimental and haunting atmosphere not too far removed from parts of *The Dreaming*).

In July 1981, Kate moved sideways to Abbey Road Studios (which then, of course, was still under the ownership of EMI), where she worked for eight weeks with engineer Haydn Bendall on 'Pull Out The Pin' and 'Night Of The Swallow', also cutting various guide vocals. Bendall later said of working with Kate, 'She taught me a huge amount about using the studio as a creative tool ... I've never really worked with any other artist quite as focused as Kate ... As far as fashioning my attitude to working with studios, I think she's one of the most important people I've ever worked with'.

Later in July, Kate travelled to Windmill Lane Studios in Dublin, Ireland, to complete 'Night Of The Swallow', recording instrumental overdubs by Irish folk groups Planxty and The Chieftains, with musical arrangement by Planxty keyboardist Bill Whelan (later the composer of the successful 1994 stage production *Riverdance*). It was a flying visit, the session lasting for a day and a night before Kate returned to the Old Smoke. Finding herself between project periods, in an effort to reinvigorate the process and refocus her ideas, a break was in order, thus the train trip to Scotland outlined at the beginning of this book.

Back home again, Hugh Padgham recommended engineer Paul Hardiman, whom Kate proceeded to work on overdubs with at Odyssey Studios near Marble Arch from August until Christmas 1981 – interrupted on 12 November by Abbey Road's 50th-anniversary party, where Kate cut the cake with British singer Helen Shapiro.

On 21 November, Kate appeared on the chat show *Friday Night Saturday Morning* with host and zoologist Dr Desmond Morris, to whom Kate revealed information that, in hindsight, seems quite remarkable. When asked where she thought her career was going, she said she anticipated a future focus on the stage and live performing – no one knowing, of course, that she would not play another full concert for a further 33 years.

Again, running out of studio time, Hardiman recommended the famous Advision Studios, which had recorded much 1960s and 1970s classic and progressive rock and had been the major recording venue for the 48-track monster *Jeff Wayne's Musical Version Of The War Of The Worlds.* Kate spoke of this period in her fan club newsletter in 1982:

> (Paul) took me around there one afternoon on a Sunday. The studio was deserted, and we went down to a small control room that proved to have a brilliant sound. We were sitting listening to tapes at full blast, and I was falling in love with the room when the door slowly opened and a rather anxious-looking studio manager edged around the door. He saw Paul, sighed with relief and explained how he'd expected a gang of thugs to be tearing up the studio while listening to tapes of their choice. As far as he had known, the studio was empty. We asked him if there would be any time for us to use the studio, and the three weeks we booked were to turn into more like three months. Paul and I were very excited about settling into one studio, and Paul had some wonderful effects for sounds that he'd put away for a rainy day. I'm pleased there was a lot of rain to come.

The four months at Advision, from January 1982 to the final mixing day of Friday 21 May, included weeks of vocal recording. They had Kate's guide vocals from the Townhouse and Abbey Road, along with some backing vocals recorded at home, but the final vocals overall were of great importance. Kate wanted to dispense with what she viewed as the lighthearted, gracious and amiable-sounding aspects of some of her vocals from the past – qualities which she felt had, at times, compromised subject matter that was more solemn or serious. She achieved this not by merely taking a more hard-edged or aggressive vocal approach in places, but by treating the voices of different song sections like characters in a play or script. She not only adopted various vocal tones to suit, but individually tailored their audible ambient environments, thereby clarifying the differing conceptual attitudes of the lyrics on a level beyond the messages themselves. This was not only from song to song but also between sections and, in many cases, from line to line. Kate told *ZigZag* magazine in 1982:

> This is the first time that I actually enjoy listening to my voice. It's a big breakthrough. Though *Never For Ever* was

> getting there, it was really a compromise all the way because I couldn't do any better at the time. I think it's the vocal cords as you get older; they do something. I can actually put some balls into my voice for the first time. It's exciting!

*This* is what Bush, Hardiman and Del Palmer were dealing with in a segment of the album production process that you might normally consider to occur in the home stretch. I'd say that, on entering Advision, the three felt like there was a *long* way to go.

And there was. Working days were an average of 15 hours long, and even during the breaks, Kate would often be working at the Fairlight. At the end of a typical day, she and Del went home, there listening to rough mixes of the day's work and figuring out what to attack the next day.

And on it went. The offers were still appearing also. In January 1982, Kate was offered a lead role in a West End production of *The Pirates Of Penzance,* which, of course, she had to turn down. (The part was eventually given to New Zealand-born actress Pamela Stephenson).

The last six weeks of production work were blighted by the Falklands War, which developed at such a rate that Palmer and Hardiman even considered whether they might be called up. Mixing of the album commenced in March.

In the end, Kate was absolutely exhausted. *The Dreaming* was finished. Whereas the otherworldly content included on the first three albums had been presented in a commercial form, there was no such concession with *The Dreaming.* The eccentric subject matter remained, but the desire to render it palatable for the public was effectively absent. The album's message? – people relentlessly inflict cruelty not only on others but themselves. This idea was reflected in the sepia-tinted album cover shot of Kate portraying Harry Houdini's wife, Bess, passing a gold key into her husband's mouth immediately prior to a life-threatening escape performance. Cruel? Perhaps. Cruel to Bess, maybe, considering Harry might die; cruel to him for the same reason. Maybe whoever is witnessing these key-passing rituals (however unknowingly) is cruel for being willing to observe the whole affair and treat it as mere entertainment, blissfully unaware or willingly ignorant of the invisible emotional tentacles. You *could* say that *that's* what was expected of anyone listening to *The Dreaming.* It must've been quite something to witness Houdini being buried alive or submerged in water. And like *The Dreaming,* it might've been difficult to quite know what to make of it – but what a hell of a show!

## The Dreaming: Personnel And Credits

Personnel as credited on the album cover:
Kate Bush: vocals, piano, CS-80, Fairlight
Geoff Downes: Fairlight
Dave Lawson: Synclavier
Stuart Elliott, Preston Hayman: drums, percussion
Paddy Bush: percussion, bullroarer, mandolin, backing vocals
Jimmy Bain, Del Palmer: bass
Danny Thompson: string bass
Eberhard Weber: upright electric bass
Ian Bairnson: guitar, backing vocals
Brian Bath, Alan Murphy: guitar
Rolf Harris: didjeridu
Liam O'Flynn: Uillean pipes, penny whistle
Sean Keane: fiddle
Donnal Lunny: bouzouki
Stewart Arnold, Dave Gilmour, Gary Hurst: backing vocals
Richard Thornton: choirboy
Percy Edwards: animals
Producer: Kate Bush
Recorded: September 1980-May 1982
Studios: The Townhouse, Abbey Road, Odyssey, Advision
Engineers: Nick Launay, Hugh Padgham, Howard Gray, George Chambers, Nick Cook (Townhouse); Haydn Bendall, Danny Dawson, John Barrett (Abbey Road); Paul Hardiman, David Taylor, Teri Reed (Odyssey, Advision)
Digital editing: Peter Woolliscroft
Mixers: Paul Hardiman and David Taylor at Advision
Cut: Ian Cooper
Photos and toning: Kindlight
Aquatinting: Nick Price
Sleeve co-ordination: Bill Clark
Eberhard Weber appears courtesy of ECM Records.

Kate's original thank you list: All at Advision and Abbey Road studios; Nigel Barker and David Woolley at Air Studios; Bob Parr and Brian Tench at Mayfair Studios; Chris Gibbons at Odyssey

Studios; Dave Gilmour, Paul Hardiman, Kay Hunter, Jim Jones, Jon Kelly, Mike King, Step Lang, Duncan McKay, Graham Middleton, Alan Murphy, Del Palmer, Steve Payne, Bill Whelan, Jay and Paddy, Ma and Pa, Lisa, Andrew, Haydn, Dan-Dan the Suchi man and to everyone who has helped to complete and inspire this album.

All lyrics © 1982, except 'Sat In Your Lap' © 1981, Kate Bush Music Ltd./EMI Music Publishing Ltd.
Label: EMI

Release date: 13 September 1982 (UK), October 1982 (US)

Chart placings: UK: 3, US: 157, CA: 29, AU: 22, DE: 23, GER: 23, NL: 5, NOR: 12, SWE: 45, JAP: 36

## 'Sat In Your Lap'

(Bush)
Released as a single A-side, 21 June 1981 (UK), b/w 'Lord Of The Reedy River'
Charts: UK: 11, AUS: 93, IRE: 18, IT: 25, NE: 32, SPA: 30
Personnel:
Kate Bush: vocals, piano, Fairlight,
Preston Hayman: drums
Jimmy Bain: bass
Geoff Downes: Fairlight CMI trumpet section
Paddy Bush: bamboo sticks, backing vocals
Preston Hayman: bamboo sticks
Ian Bairnson, Gary Hurst, Stewart Arnold: backing vocals

It's quite surprising how much the 'Sat In Your Lap' demo sounds like the prior Kate Bush material. The demo's vocal style was as-yet unaltered, other than a dour tone adopted for a few lines. By and large, you're hearing the cute, innocent soprano of a song like 'Kashka From Baghdad' (*Lionheart,* 1979). Not that Kate hadn't experimented with vocal tone before. On that very album, the following song, 'Coffee Homeground', was perhaps her first real excursion into varied vocal theatrics within one piece and a successful experiment it *was,* too. In fact, that song (perhaps in a modified arrangement technology-wise and made bereft of its German cabaret affectation) could've sat quite comfortably in the lap of *The Dreaming* and would've probably been its most accessible and understandable song, in contrast with being its parent album's most difficult and obscure. 'Coffee Homeground' is a good pointer to Kate's wish to develop artistically without limitation towards what she became on *The Dreaming.*

Another noticeable aspect of the 'Sat In Your Lap' demo is the fact that the arrangement really wasn't finished, which is fine and even expected, of course: it *was* a demo after all. But considering its eccentric complexity, you can understand why Hugh Padgham bowed out; faced with the possibility of all the material being presented with an unfinished arrangement suggested a long road ahead.

But a most remarkable aspect of the song's birth was its inspiration – the Stevie Wonder concert Kate had been to at Wembley the night before. She said the song was 'inspired by the feeling of his music'. If that's the case, it's absolutely impossible to tell. And rightly so – Bush was no exponent of cookie-cutter music. Her way was clearly to soak up inspiration, adding it to the cauldron as it were, and letting it come out if it happened to or not. Kate and her musical brethren of the era were bound by no such necessities as perfect rhyme scheme, prosody (reflecting lyric ideas musically) or any of what some might've considered to be dusty old rules laid down by the greats of the preceding 200 years (but mostly the preceding 50 or so). But that's not to say she wasn't aware and didn't have an eye on such things – which was made clear from the 'Sat In Your Lap' line, 'My cup, she never overfloweth', which ran slightly longer than the lines in the same position in neighbouring verses. Even then, she lengthened it more out of irony than straight prosody, which would've been too transparent if anyone had even noticed: more irony. You don't find that stuff in Stevie Wonder songs.

Being album four, Bush's music was now mature enough to rule out any possibility of her being the deer-in-the-headlights of overt influence. Rather than start from scratch with some Stevie-flavoured chords, she took a piano chord pattern she already had, laid it against a drum machine rhythm and came up with a verse melody and some words. Cleverly, the Wonder inspiration was merely in the air and not overtly in the music. She recorded the chorus vocals first ('Some say that knowledge is...'), as the verses were still incomplete. In fact, the introductory first verse was omitted from the final master recording, which began with what used to be the second verse ('I see the people working...').

When the time came to record the master at Townhouse Studio Two, the Roland TR-808 rhythm box was recorded accompanying live piano. The 808 was later replaced by drummer Preston Hayman, utilising the cavernous Townhouse drum sound already familiar from Peter Gabriel's 'Intruder' and Phil Collins' 'In The Air Tonight', though, this time – at least audibly – minus the recognisable signature gate that had insinuated itself so accidentally into those records at the hands of Hugh Padgham's skill. If anything, the seemingly gateless 'Sat In Your Lap' drum sound might've influenced Padgham's towering drum ambience recorded on XTC's *English Settlement* album at Richard Branson's Manor Studio in Oxfordshire several months later. I say 'seemingly' because, at this point in recording history, gates were used on virtually everything all the time – certainly on drums – to control leakage of other instruments that may be playing live alongside them. The gate would automatically mute, say, a snare track (for example) after every snare hit had finished sounding. As a result, anything on the snare track that was below a certain decibel level (leaking instruments, noise floor) would not be heard, therefore not conflating the mixing process later. If a drum had analog or digital reverb on it, that reverb would usually come after the gate in the chain so that only the snare (and not leakage because it was no longer there) was reverberated. In a case where the gate was chained after the reverb effect – encapsulating it – the gate would merely be set wide so as to only mute the track when the reverb tail had finished sounding. This could be applied to acoustic room reverb, too, which, of course, means the gate came after it in the chain. Accidentally setting the gate too far closed in that situation is how the 'Intruder'/'In The Air Tonight' drum sound was discovered – the gate cut the sound off before the reverb had finished sounding, causing that sudden ending on all the drum sounds. It would've been so easy to just close that gate a little more to virtually replicate the 'In The Air Tonight' drum sound on 'Sat In Your Lap' (though, to be fair, the kind of drums Phil Collins used – and the way they were tuned and mic'ed – would've had a lot to do with it), but my guess would be that Kate stopped short of copping an obvious trend – which, of course, was her all over.

Keen to get her new sound out into the world, Kate choreographed a routine and filmed a video for 'Sat In Your Lap', rush-releasing the single (b/w the Donovan song 'Lord

Of The Reedy River') on 21 June: a pivotal point in her career. The single peaked highest in the UK, where it reached 11, which was pretty good considering it was an intellectual piece contemplating the whys and wherefores of human effort versus lack of motivation: not exactly chart fodder. But it was to be another three years before she again hit the top 20.

The 7"-vinyl runout was etched with the words 'WELL DONE J.B. FIRST DAN', which presumably was for Kate's brother John Carder Bush (also known as Jay), who took the cover photograph.

The album version was a slight remix, with louder, clearer vocals and, in some spots, louder synthesizer brass – a part which came courtesy of Geoff Downes (formerly of Buggles, Yes and soon to be part of British supergroup Asia). The recording was also completed quicker than any of the album's other tracks and was the only one contained within one 24-track tape, the rest of the album using 48 – in actuality, *47* tracks, as, in such a case, one track always had to be taken up with time code to synchronise the two 24-track tape recorders. This was fairly standard stuff by 1982, with 48 tracks first being utilised in the making of *Jeff Wayne's Musical Version Of The War Of The Worlds.* However, again, it was The Beatles that first used such a technique when, in 1967, they synced two four-track recorders together for the (seven-track) recording of *Sgt. Pepper's Lonely Hearts Club Band.*

The 'Sat In Your Lap' video was shot with director Brian Wiseman over two days in June 1982. The long shots were filmed at Abbey Road Studio Two – this being perhaps the first music video in history where that floor was one of the stars of the show. And there was plenty more to like visually, not the least of which was the lovely blue sci-fi vortex, Kate's beautifully choreographed Flamenco dancing, and most of all, the book sitting in her lap that unexpectedly flies away.

## 'There Goes A Tenner'

(Bush)
Released as a single A-side, 29 October 1982 (UK), b/w 'Ne T'en Fui Pas'
Personnel:
Kate Bush: vocals, piano, Fairlight, CS-80
Stuart Elliott: drums
Del Palmer: bass
Dave Lawson: Synclavier

The album's third single was perhaps the first (semi) high-profile UK song about a robbery since Genesis' 'Robbery, Assault And Battery' in 1976 (*A Trick Of The Tail)*. One theory I saw about 'There Goes A Tenner' suggested that the robber's paranoia about his ability to complete the task was, in fact, a metaphor for Kate's possible insecurity around having the last say on all aspects of an album production. I'd say that would be pushing it – far too much is read into these things far too often. We know autobiography-in-song is extremely rare in Kate's case. I've always found the song to be funny, as it reminds me of the hilarious *Monty Python's Flying Circus* 1970 skit about The Piranha Brothers, who were a kind of bumbling version of the Kray twins.

Beyond all of that, the track contains one of the album's most achingly beautiful musical passages – Del Palmer's fretless bass and harmonics against Kate's atmospheric CS-80 synth chords in the two virtually instrumental 12-bar sections (0:44 and 1:51). The sections are so seductive that it's a disappointment when the jolly Cockney-sounding verse returns immediately afterwards, however well-arranged the Synclavier brass of Dave Lawson (ex of British progressive rock band Greenslade) may be. What's more, in defence of all the verses, we *do* get the gated reverb technique – not on the drums, but on the lead vocal. It's a complex effect here, the reverb appearing to gate/mute itself even before a vocal line ends – a virtual mirror image of the famous gated drum sound, which *did* have a reverb tail, even though it was suddenly cut off.

'There Goes A Tenner' was the first Kate Bush single to chart only in the UK, where it reached a mere 93. Issued on 29 October 1982, the B-side was Kate's love song 'Ne T'en Fui Pas'.

The video, directed by Paul Henry (who'd also directed the video for 'The Dreaming'), lacked the more-instant appeal of the two prior single videos ('Sat In Your Lap' and 'The Dreaming'), though Del Palmer's inclusion as the getaway driver was interesting, and the M. C. Escher-esque imagery of the robbers gazing into a floor hole at a giant clock pendulum swinging horizontally was a high point.

## 'Pull Out The Pin'

(Bush)
Personnel:
Kate Bush: vocals, piano
Preston Hayman: drums
Danny Thompson: string bass
Brian Bath: guitar:
Dave Gilmour: backing vocals

The idea behind 'Pull Out The Pin' came from the 1979 documentary *Front Line,* which showed Australian cameraman Neil Davis on the front lines in Vietnam, showing everything from the Vietnamese point of view. In November 1982, Kate spoke in depth about the song to *ZigZag* magazine:

> He said it really changed him because, until you live on their level like that – when it's complete survival – you don't know what it's about. He's never been the same since because it's so devastating, people dying all the time. The way he portrayed the Vietnamese was as this really crafted, beautiful race. The Vietnamese could smell (the Americans) coming for miles because of the tobacco and cologne. It was devastating because you got the impression that the Americans were so heavy and awkward, and the Vietnamese were so beautiful and all getting wiped out. They wore a little silver Buddha on a chain around their neck, and when they went into action, they'd pop it into their mouth so if they died, they'd have Buddha on their lips. I wanted to write a song that could somehow convey the whole thing, so we set it in the jungle and had helicopters, crickets and little Balinese frogs.

The Buddha in the mouth corresponds with the album cover shot portraying Harry Houdini's wife Bess, with the padlock key in her mouth. The lyric concept as a whole recalls the war-torn single 'Army Dreamers' of *Never For Ever,* though 'Pull Out The Pin' is much more intense.

The lyric perspective is from a Vietnamese soldier stalking his American prey for days until the two come face-to-face.

But alas, there's 'just one thing in it: me or him'. Overall, the lyric is slightly impenetrable in as much as the verses suffer moments of oscillation between the past and present tense, making things, at times, nonsensical:

Just as we hit the green
I've never been so happy to be alive
Only seven miles behind
You could smell the child
The smell of the front line's survival

I had not seen his face
'Til I'm only feet away

This isn't helped by poor rhythmic syllable stressing like 'AmeRIcan' instead of 'aMErican'. A slight rhythmic adjustment in the singing could've avoided that; it wasn't necessarily a writing fault.

The track was recorded at Abbey Road with engineer Haydn Bendall, whom Kate had first met when she sang on the Roy Harper album *The Unknown Soldier* (1980). The voice of Pink Floyd's David Gilmour is clearly recognisable on the choruses – his first actual appearance on a Kate Bush record despite him being executive producer of *The Kick Inside.*

From the outset, the star of 'Pull Out The Pin' is Danny Thompson's exquisite double bass playing (despite what sounds like an accidental filter or EQ move at 0:44 removing the bass' low-end frequencies for a moment, returning halfway through the note underneath the line 'Living on your belly') in conjunction with Kate's jazz-like piano chords. Thompson was previously a member of Pentangle and Alexis Korner's Blues Incorporated, having become an in-demand session player for everyone from Nick Drake to Mary Hopkin, John Martyn and beyond. I'd go as far as to suggest that the texture heard here on 'Pull Out The Pin' was absolutely clocked by musician David Sylvian of the UK group Japan in advance of his solo debut *Brilliant Trees,* recorded in 1983. Not that such a texture hadn't been heard before, with 'Pull Out The Pin' sounding stylistically similar to music released by German jazz label ECM – its artist bass player Eberhard Weber appeared later on *The Dreaming*.

The track is audibly interesting throughout (if not always sonically pristine), including guitarist Brian Bath's almost-heavy-metal distorted guitar line on the chorus, his angular harmony on the largely instrumental middle section and what he later described as his 'ridiculous diminished guitar lick, which just went all over the place, like a Jimmy Bryant thing' over the closing section.

The passing-car sound effect in verse two was probably an unnecessary use of a stock Fairlight sample (quite a few of which we'd already heard on *Never For Ever* when the Fairlight was still a novelty ('All We Ever Look For')). More impressive are the percussive and melodic Fairlight components – most clear in the introduction – with their characteristic glassy quality. A major effect used later in the track was the sound of helicopter rotor blades, which drummer Preston Hayman had recorded on cassette when visiting the Indonesian island of Bali. Not a Fairlight sound at all, it's tempting to hear the rotor-blade sounds as the rhythmic basis for the closing section, which they do actually appear to be for eight bars or so before increasing in speed and fading out earlier than the textural, avant-garde background still moving at the piece's locked-in tempo.

The multiple screams of 'I love life!' towards the end are possibly the album's most aggressive utterance, though oddly, they were EQ'ed and panned in such a way as to have minimal impact. The hard panning suggests two voices – one each on the left and right. But it's actually just one voice – on the right, with the left side being a digital delay of the right side (with added reverb). Panning is always a good way to adjust degrees of intensity, and perhaps it was used here so that the 'I love life!' wasn't too annoying – although, for it to be overly annoying would've been highly appropriate. Even so, the multiple repeats were irritating enough for David Gilmour's

**Above:** Kate poses in the studio, September 1982. (*Alamy*)

**Above:** The front cover of *The Dreaming* ...

**Below:** ... and the back. (*EMI*)

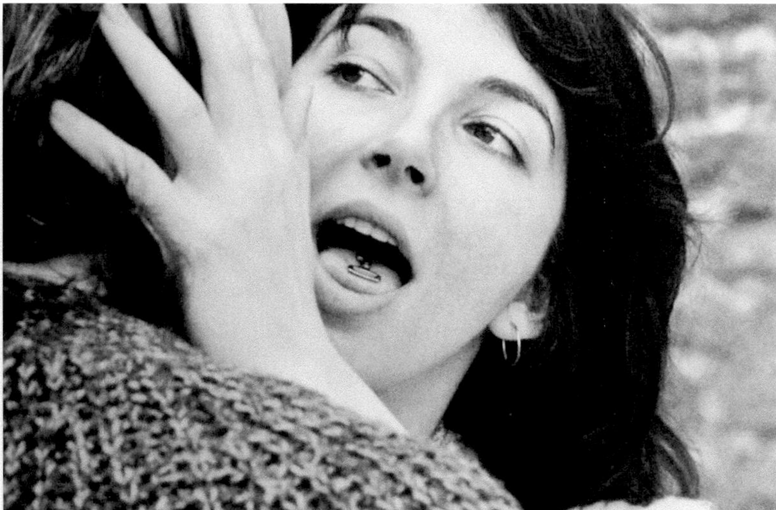

**Above:** A test shot for the front cover. (*John Carder Bush*)

**Below:** A colour outtake from the shoot for the front cover. (*John Carder Bush*)

**Above:** Kate and colourful jesters in the video for 'Sat In Your Lap'.

**Below:** Just when she thinks she's King in the 'Sat In Your Lap' video.

**Above:** Wide-eyed in the 'There Goes A Tenner' video.

**Below:** Flanked by accomplices in the 'There Goes A Tenner' robbery.

**Above:** Kate and dancers in the video for 'The Dreaming'. (*Alamy*)

**Above:** A close-up of the David Bowie 'Ashes To Ashes' costume worn in 'The Dreaming'.

**Below:** Bush appears like a 1930s Hollywood starlet in the video for 'The Dreaming'.

**Above:** Bush signing albums for fans at the Virgin Megastore in London on 14 September 1982. (*Peter Still/Redferns*)

final multi-voice utterance of 'Pull out the pin' at 4:05 to sound like the last wish of a man who knows the satisfaction of the request might very well kill him.

## 'Suspended In Gaffa'

(Bush)
Released as a single A-side, 1982, b/w 'Dreamtime (Instrumental)' (FRA)/'Ne T'Eu Fui Pas' (GER/NE/SPA)
Released as a single A-side, January 1983 (AUS), b/w 'Ne T'Eu Fui Pas'
Released as a single B-side, January 1983 (CAN), b/w 'Un Baiser D'Enfant (The Infant Kiss)'
Charts: FRA: 33, NE: 50, SPA: 38
Personnel:
Kate Bush: vocals, piano, strings
Stuart Elliott: drums and sticks
Del Palmer: bass
Paddy Bush: strings, mandolins
Dave Lawson: Synclavier

The lyric for the album's fourth single (released only in Europe and Australia) was completed unusually early in the songwriting process. Kate explained the lyric's meaning in her fan club newsletter:

> The idea of the song is that of being given a glimpse of God – something that we dearly want – but being told that, unless we work for it, we will never see it again, and even then, we might not be worthy of it. Of course, everybody wants the reward without the toil, so people try to find a way out of the hard work, still hoping to claim the prize, but such is not the case.

This theme of laziness aligns with that of 'Sat In Your Lap'. In 1982, Kate revealed to *The Guardian* that 'Suspended In Gaffa' was...

> ...reasonably autobiographical, which most of my songs aren't. It's about seeing something that you want, on any level, and not being able to get that thing ... and then when you achieve it, you enter a different level – everything will slightly change ... But when you explain it like this, it doesn't

sound like anything. The idea is much more valuable within the song than it is in me telling you about it. When you analyse it, it seems silly.

The stream-of-consciousness lyric – which Kate claimed to have trouble singing due to the lack of an opportunity to breathe over the first few phrases – is actually one of this album's most finely constructed, rhythmically. It rolls off the tongue like butter if you're familiar with the piece's movement:

Out in the garden
There's half of a heaven
And we're only bluffing
We're not ones for busting through walls
But they've told us
Unless we can prove that we're doing it
We can't have it all
He's gonna wangle
A way to get out of it
She's an excuse and a witness who'll talk when he's called
But they've told us
Unless we can prove that we're doing it
We can't have it all

The narrator certainly sounds like they're in a hurry, considering the lyric's theme of laziness. Enlivening the fast waltz was Kate's brother, Paddy Bush. In fact, this recording was a real showcase for his magnificent, dexterous mandolin playing. In the original album liner notes, the strings were credited to both Paddy and Kate. The instrumental sections after each verse are *almost* equal in beauty to the post-verse sections in 'There Goes A Tenner'.

The single's highest chart position was 33 in France, and the accompanying Brian-Wiseman-directed music video appeared to have the lowest budget of all for this album. That's not to say it wasn't of value. It consisted solely of Kate in a barn, miming and dancing, with nil in the way of special effects other than the final moment where she disappears into an outside wall, achieved – it looks like – via a simple cross-fade. But the visual substance was in the dancing. Much of her choreography betrayed a most postmodern influence, here incorporating seeming motifs, postures, poses and gestures resembling anything from the most basic moves that anyone could do, to the S-shape face-outline mime of Marcel Marceau, to subtle disco hip thrusts, to the complex angular shapes and jumps of Russian Vaslav Najinsky's groundbreaking 1913 work on Stravinsky's *Le Sacre Du Printemps* (*The Rite Of Spring*) for the Ballets Russes. This was all channelled through what Kate had learnt from an earlier period of personal tutelage from British dancer/choreographer Lindsay Kemp. When it came to dancing, Bush was clearly a prodigy. It was all in there and – like her music – had a clear depth of purpose exceeding the medium itself. In fact, there's an argument that Kate's music, in general, was/is sometimes difficult for some because it's probably best taken in conjunction with the visual aspect. Kate Bush was a multimedia artist long before the term shifted into the common vernacular. By 1982, it was all just one big lump of artistic stuff for Bush, who was in that period of development that so few are lucky enough to reach – where she'd seemingly forgotten everything she knew and was running on sheer instinct: nice work if you can get anywhere near it, and dangerous for the competition.

## 'Leave It Open'

(Bush)
Personnel:
Kate Bush: vocals, piano, Fairlight
Preston Hayman: drums
Jimmy Bain: bass
Alan Murphy: electric guitar
Ian Bairnson: acoustic guitar

'Leave It Open' was the first demo worked on at the beginning with Hugh Padgham at the Townhouse. Kate said in the fan club newsletter: 'This song is about being open and shut to stimuli at the right times. Often, we have closed minds and open mouths when perhaps we should have open minds and shut mouths.'

Instrumentally, the strident medium-tempo track is fairly minimalist until the low-fi Fairlight strings make their entrance in verse two. Considering the lyric is probably the album's most easily interpreted so far, the sheer amount of vocal effects (electronic or otherwise: from breathing to throat-clearing to screaming) make comprehension difficult at times. 'Leave It Open' is a good example of the technique whereby different sections or individual lines were performed in various vocal tones and individually affected as if they were different characters in a story. The initial vocal character states, 'With my ego in my gut/My babbling mouth would wash it up', in an ironic, seemingly conflicted and almost non-caring manner, followed by the diametrically opposed, 'But now I've started learning how', in a youthful, virtuous, even naive characterisation. The initial character then returns with, 'I keep it, *shut*'. I say 'returning' and not 'responding', as that first character seems to be completely unaware of the second, though the second may not be unaware of the first: the conscience speaking, perhaps. Theoretically, it's the first character saying all of it. It's heady stuff, indeed. Songwriting and the perception of lyric content had certainly come a long way in the 30 years since Patti Page's 1953 hit '(How Much Is) That Doggie In The Window?'. (There's also an argument for suggesting it really hasn't progressed much further in the 42 years since *The Dreaming* was recorded).

Now, let's turn to the elephant in the room – the backwards vocals at the end. Anyone who visited the studio during the album sessions was played this song's closing vocal section to see if they could guess what words were being sung, Kate later claiming, 'It is very difficult to guess, but it can be done, especially when you know what the song is about.' This has been a mystery since the beginning, and there are many incorrect assumptions on the internet as to what Kate was actually singing on those closing lines. The popular interpretation seems to be 'We let the weirdness in', and that's where it has sat for years. It's worth taking an objective look at this issue, though I can't promise an absolutely definitive answer.

The first time I heard the line in question back in the 1980s, it was immediately obvious that the vocals were running backwards. The reversal was clear from the altered sibilance and totally obvious from the reverb tail sucking up *before* the words appeared. Paddy Bush has claimed that Kate wanted to sing the words (believed to be 'We let the weirdness in'), but worked out the phonetics in reverse and sang those reversed phonetics before reversing *that* forwards recording, thus the audio appearing in reverse, the words then intelligible. Now we *think* we know what it's saying. But Paddy's theory could be a red herring because when you play 'Leave It Open' backwards, on the line in question, you hear actual words sung normally, not phoney phonetics, which always sound unnaturally awkward if pieced together and spoken.

Dismissing Paddy's explanation, what we have is simply a backwards recording of a line that sounds a lot like 'We let the weirdness in'. So played in reverse (the correct way around), what is she actually saying? The popular interpretation of the reverse audio appears to be 'They say we were buried here'. However, the left and right consist of different vocal recordings, which also seem to differ in some consonant sounds. One possibility could be 'And they said they want the reveal', which could really be quite the in-joke if Bush and co.

were predicting a possible level of ongoing discussion on the subject. There is also the possibility that the ending lines in question were flown in from a completely different song. It's the kind of thing that was sometimes done in a situation like this, though I find no evidence of what that song might be. It's certainly nothing on *The Dreaming*.

This all rakes up the issue of so-called 'back-masking' – an ambiguous term at best, as it suggests some kind of skulduggery or deception at work. The correct terminology is merely 'backwards audio'. Yes, people often reversed audio in their recordings, but the times it was in an effort to disguise something were minimal. Besides, surely the best way to disguise something would be to leave it out altogether. Backwards audio was just a bit of fun, and the joke was on those who took it seriously.

The first widely-known commercial recording to include an aspect of reversed audio was The Beatles' May 1966 B-side 'Rain', which contained a reversed recording of John Lennon singing – the idea occurring to him when he accidentally played the track backwards. The Beatles did more audio reversal over the years, as did many others, but the technique was never thought of as a problem until 1982 when America's Trinity Broadcasting Network retrospectively accused Led Zeppelin of using 'Stairway To Heaven' to subliminally communicate Satanic messages. Other back-masking accusations poured forth from various sources – one of the most ridiculous being levelled at the Electric Light Orchestra's 1974 track 'Eldorado'. ELO leader Jeff Lynne responded by recording 'Fire On High', with its Hammer Films-style introduction featuring a low voice, which, upon reversal, revealed itself to be saying, 'The music is reversible, but time is not. Turn back', as if the voice's owner was looking down on the audio investigator so studiously sitting at his record player trying to wind the turntable backwards.

This information renders it appropriate for me to now correct my statement in this book's introduction where I claimed that no further connection could be made between Kate Bush and Aleister Crowley. One conceptual allegiance *can* be mined when you consider that Crowley's 1913 book *Magick (Book 4)* contained advice for the achievement of backwards thinking by listening to phonograph records in reverse – though you could say that Kate Bush and others took it a step further by actually creating records for those backwards-thinking explorers to listen to. Clearly, reversed audio took up her thinking for a short time, and she may indeed have conducted the long-winded phonetic experiment as proposed by Paddy Bush. If so, why did Kate not turn it into a thing? Why did she leave it at just this one solitary example in the case of *The Dreaming*? I'd say, for two reasons, though, running on instinct as she did, I doubt she really voiced them even as thought sentences – firstly, it had already been done (sheer anathema), and secondly, it was a lot of trouble to go to for little-to-no reward. (She probably *did* voice that last reason).

## 'The Dreaming'

(Bush)
Released as a single A-side, 23 July 1982 (UK), b/w 'Dreamtime (Instrumental Version)'
Charts: UK: 48, AUS: 91
Personnel:
Kate Bush: vocals, piano, Fairlight
Stuart Elliott: drums
Rolf Harris: didjeridu
Percy Edwards: animals
Paddy Bush: bullroarer, backing vocals
Gosfield Goers: crowd

The idea of writing and recording a song with an Australian concept arose back in 1980 during the recording of *Never For Ever*. Kate later said she was glad it didn't manifest until afterwards, as it wouldn't have sounded the same. The track's basis was the same as Australian Rolf Harris' George-Martin-produced 1961 hit 'Sun Arise', its rhythm reproduced here with a LinnDrum.

The lyric is about the plight of Australia's Aborigines, which Kate had been reading about in a book on Australian lore. She explained in a 1982 fan-club newsletter:

> This song had to try and convey the wide-open bush, the Aborigines – it had to roll around in mud and dirt, try to become a part of the earth. 'Earthy' was the word used most to explain the sounds. There was a flood of imagery waiting to be painted into the song – the Aborigines move away as the digging machines move in, mining for ore and plutonium; their sacred grounds are destroyed.

Kate prepared a didjeridu drone on the Fairlight (effectively the track's bass part) and invited Rolf Harris to come and replace the part with a real didjeridu. English animal impersonator Percy Edwards also contributed, playing the aural parts of sheep, dingoes and magpies.

The song needed a title. 'Dreamtime' was a possibility (ultimately used for the single B-side mix), which was the name the Aborigines gave to a religious time when humans and animals took on the same form. Also known as the dreaming, the concept became the song title, though the phrase wasn't uttered within the recording itself. But the word 'Dreamtime' *was*, to an extent – broken into its constituent syllables in backing vocals between verses. But the term was definitely sung on the B-side 'Dreamtime', which suggests it was recorded before the final title had been found. Last to go on was the car-door slam in the album's later sessions.

Kate had made it clear she was looking for ways to alter the sound of her voice – not with effects necessarily, but in the style of singing. She managed to do this on the album while still sounding original for the most part. But in the case of this song, the seeming influence of British singer Toyah Wilcox is unmistakable. Kate later said that the album seemed to desperately cry, 'I'm an artist!'. But she could've afforded to cut herself some slack, as – considering this track *is* one of the album's most characteristically odd – the recording is perhaps the album's most transparent. This is thanks not only to the seeming Toyah reference as a pop-culture touchstone but also to the clear conception. From the didjeridu drone to the Australian accent to the clear narrative presence of the Aborigine plight, it's pretty obvious from the first listen what the whole thing is about: not something many other *Dreaming* tracks could be accused of. The track is also quite understandable musically. Unlike other tracks here, it basically sits on one chord – or at least one drone acting as a bass note, with chordal variations moving around it – therefore being less harmonically demanding on the listener, as if to musically suggest a long, flat journey across the desert. By basically handing the listener a completely understandable piece of work, the only decision left for them to make was whether they actually liked it or not – and therein lay the crux of the biscuit and a slice of uniformity for Kate Bush music in general: its ability to polarise. And that flips my theory on its head, as, considering the entire concept was so easily comprehended, the track *can* be quite a difficult listen for some. But that kind of contradiction is Bush all over. The track's ambiguity makes it as historically relevant as the music of eclectic pioneers like Charles Ives or Alfred Schnittke – their entire *modus operandi* being to obliterate the borders between high and low art: 'even if I break my neck in doing so', in the case of Schnittke. Kate Bush here obliterated those borders effortlessly and most likely unknowingly.

Considering 'The Dreaming' was so original, it bore another conventional element in the Fairlight orchestra-hit sample known as ORCH5, which had become familiar from the Afrika Bambaataa & the Soul Sonic Force hit 'Planet Rock', released just three months before the 'The Dreaming' single (which came two months prior to its own album). Admittedly, to adopt a trend was abnormal for the usually-cutting-edge Bush, and in 'The Dreaming', the sample *is* largely untreated, low in volume and fairly subtle, as if played down. (It is first clearly audible at 0:17, though it is much clearer throughout the second verse). Still, as stated earlier, some tracks on *The Dreaming* made no secret of the then-popular Townhouse drum sound. So, taking those two trends into account, perhaps over time, *The Dreaming* – often identified as Bush's most original work – has come to be considered secondary in innovation to the fiercely original (and more accessible) *Hounds Of Love* (1985), which, in hindsight, doesn't shout any contemporary sonic trends too loudly at all: food for thought. The two albums probably vie for superiority in the Bush canon, but in the end, it comes down to a matter of taste.

However, the track 'The Dreaming' *was* clearly more innovative than accessible thanks to its interesting sonics, such as the steely guitar/piano textures against the aural background (the result of work at the Townhouse with Nick Launay) and the impressive vocal effects, extended via Fairlight looping and reverb, heard clearly on the phrase 'See the light' at 3:11.

The video – conceived by Kate Bush and co-directed with Paul Henry – was bedecked as if taking place in the Australian outback within view of Ayers Rock, presumably in the period of Dreamtime. Like Brian Wiseman's 'Suspended In Gaffa' video, the choreography runs the style gamut, with allusions to everything from the Disney character Tinkerbell, bird flight and the sans-gravity slow motion of walking on the Moon, to the Limbo dance and even moves resembling popular 1970s/1980s British dance troupe Hot Gossip.

Three accompanying dancers adorned in tribal face paint wear costumes that are darker but similar in style to the white boilersuit-like space suit with protruding hose worn by Kate. Incidentally, her costume was virtually as much a star of the show as she was. The suit had an interesting history, with David Bowie having worn it in parts of his 1980 'Ashes To Ashes' video (where it's seen quite clearly at 2:23). British record producer Rupert Hine wore the suit more obviously in certain scenes of the video for his 1981 single 'Misplaced Love' (unmistakable at 2:07). Kate wears the suit throughout her video, making its identification easy, characterised as it was by winding seams in a design not unlike those of old *Doctor Who* episodes, where particular creatures' skins were clearly made from cloth – indeed, the background of the 'The Dreaming' video could cause you to expect the sudden appearance of a Dalek over a *papier-mâché* ridge!

The video's final tasteful touch was the buried face protruding from the sand, which had the last enigmatic word – an audio moment that lacked potency minus the visual aspect.

The first run of promo 7" singles were under the title 'The Abo Song' before being recalled and the song retitled. But sadly, as 'The Dreaming', the single (with cover art by Del Palmer) struggled to secure airplay. BBC Radio 1 straight-out refused to play it, and the single halted at 48 in the UK. Furthermore, in an age when virtually all 7" singles had a 12" sibling, EMI outright rejected the possibility of a 12", viewing the idea as not viable in this case. So much for market forces and the wisdom of corporate decision-making. 'The Dreaming' is a substantial recording, notwithstanding.

## 'Night Of The Swallow'

(Bush)
Released as a single A-side, 25 November 1983(IRE), b/w 'Houdini'
Personnel:
Kate Bush: vocals, piano, Fairlight
Stuart Elliott: drums
Del Palmer: fretless and 8-string bass
Liam O'Flynn: Uillean pipes and penny whistle
Sean Keane: fiddle
Donnal Lunny: bouzouki
Pipes and strings written and arranged by Bill Whelan

This first track recorded at Abbey Road with engineer Haydn Bendall ended up being quite a complex production, taking full advantage of the facility's studios, also requiring a location shift to Windmill Lane studio in Dublin, Ireland, to record the Irish ensemble. As an example of the complexity, drummer Stuart Elliott's performance in Abbey Road studio 3 was played through speakers in studio 1, where the large hall's reverberation was fed back and recorded through the mixing desk in studio 2.

When writing the song, Kate had thought a ceilidh band would be ideal for the choruses – as in the kind of small group of Irish players that might sit around playing at an informal gathering. Being a fan of traditional Irish group Planxty, Kate called keyboard player Bill Whelan and asked him to do an arrangement for the song. Bill agreed to take it on, and within a few days of receiving a cassette of the track, he called back and – as a demonstration – he and pipe player Liam O'Flynn played along with the cassette there and then right down the phone line.

It was then arranged for Kate and her brother John to make a flying visit to Dublin to record the arrangement with the players at Windmill Lane. Kate spoke of the session in her fan club newsletter:

> As the choruses began to grow, the evening drew on and the glasses of Guinness – slowly dropping in level – became like sandglasses to tell the passing of time. We missed our

> plane and worked through the night. By eight o'clock the next morning, we were driving to the airport to return to London. I had a very precious tape tucked under my arm, and just as we were stepping onto the plane, I looked up into the sky and there were three swallows diving and chasing the flies.

With the straight piano, bass and drums of the verses, this is the *Dreaming* track that sounds most like her earlier material – indeed, the rhythm section of Kate, drummer Stuart Elliott and bassist Del Palmer had populated the majority of *Lionheart.* With its semi-progressive air and time-signature changes moving from the slow verse 4/4 to the chorus' moderate 12/8 jig, this track was/is a creature seemingly more of the late-period bell-bottom than the early-era digital crucible.

The 'Night Of The Swallow' lyric was, of course, as worthy as *any* on *The Dreaming.* In fact, along with the track's singing, the lyric is probably the album's most traditional, not to mention the album's clearest, along with the title track. Traditionally in pop, the most direct tracks were usually reserved for side one of an album, to help draw listeners in. But Kate wasn't like everyone else. She had no intention of making any commercial concession or compromise for *The Dreaming* whatsoever. So, on an album full of cutting-edge lyrics, the more traditional 'Night Of The Swallow' appropriately fell short with its unforeseen changes of narrative voice. The verses showcase a female begging her pilot partner not to fly out on an illegal job:

> Oh, please don't go through with this
> I don't like the sound of it

Suddenly, the chorus features the male character justifying his actions, though the perspective change isn't made clear:

> Before you know
> I'll be over the water like a swallow

And I'm home before the morning

In its defence, at least that ambiguity was a good fit with the rest of the album's material. And, of course, Kate wasn't here to satisfy any cookie-cutter cravings. There *is* an argument that this song might've worked better as a duet with a male – perhaps Peter Gabriel, whose high tenor could've served the concept well while giving the choruses a satisfying urgency (perhaps with some necessary uppermost-melody adjustment to accommodate the lower male vocal range).

One version of the lyric on the internet had the closing last line, 'But you're not a swallow'. This would've made a great coda to the story, though it's not heard on the recording.

In 1983, 'Night Of The Swallow' was issued as a single in Ireland only, but it failed to chart – perhaps thanks to the absence of a video and the presence of poor label promotion.

## 'All The Love'

(Bush)
Personnel:
Kate Bush: vocals, piano, Fairlight
Stuart Elliott: drums
Del Palmer: fretless bass
Richard Thornton: choirboy

The album's most simple production is quite possibly also its most poignant. The minimal accompaniment of piano, bass, drums and subtle Fairlight samples renders 'All The Love' as the most direct track here. The sonic space allows the harmonic overtones of Del Palmer's fretless bass to ring clearly – completely worthy of recordings heard on Manfred Eichers' German record label ECM, the motto of which was 'The most beautiful sound next to silence': 'All The Love' could certainly be accused of fitting that description. Indeed, ECM recording artist and bass player Eberhard Weber plays electric upright on the following track 'Houdini', and the masterful delicacy of his playing would've also perfectly suited 'All The Love', though Del Palmer's engaging bass part here must be viewed as indispensable and amongst his finest recorded work.

Fretless bass (sometimes with octaver, but more often with a chorus effect plastered over it) became quite trendy in pop recordings for a few years in the early 1980s, the precedent being mostly the gorgeous and unignorable playing of Mick Karn from British group Japan. Karn was the next best thing after Jaco Pastorius – at least in pop – and had few competitors. Roxy Music's Alan Spenner was a definite contender, though he had his own style focussed more on tone, keeping slides to a minimum.

Ultimately, the fretless-pop crown went to Welshman Pino Palladino, who, after playing all over Gary Numan's mighty 1982 album *I, Assassin,* seemed to appear on every second record that came out. This continued for several years, arguably peaking in quality with Palladino's elegantly ravishing additions to Don Henley's stunning 1985 single

'Sunset Grill'. The trend was such that, at times, you'd buy a record just for the bass playing, though it must be said that there was plenty of quality songwriting accompanying those seductive fretless bass parts.

Kate talked about the meaning of 'All The Love' in a fan club newsletter in 1982:

> Although we are often surrounded by people and friends, we are all ultimately alone, and I feel sure everyone feels lonely at some time in their life. I wanted to write about feeling alone and how having to hide emotions away or being too scared to show love, can lead to being lonely.

It is quite a confronting lyric when you read it on the cold light of the page:

> The first time I died
> Was in the arms of good friends of mine
> They kiss me with tears
> They hadn't been near me for years
> Say, why do it now when I won't be around?
> I'm going out

The first time around, the voice of the choirboy plays the role of the collective voice of the friends being addressed:

> We needed you to love us too
> We wait for your move

Alongside the choirboy's voice are the kind of monosyllabic Fairlight vocal samples you would've heard on tracks of the period by Swiss electronic act Yello, who made a feature of such vocal snatches. But the semi-humourous-sounding syllables sit almost incongruously against the pure and serious choirboy vocal here.

Verse two goes no easier on the friends, as the narrator turns to admit to the listener:

Only tragedy allows the release
Of love and grief never normally seen
I didn't want to let them see me weep
I didn't want to let them see me weak
But I know I have shown
That I stand at the gates alone

But this time, the choirboy follows ambiguously, either in the character of the main narrator or as just one of the friends:

I needed you to love me too
I wait for your move

Oddly, after this second choirboy section, the piano appears to enter a bit early as it proceeds to the first chorus. It's slightly frustrating, but when the exact same thing happens later going into the second chorus, the only conclusion that can be drawn is that a purposeful (but completely unnecessary) bar of 7/8 exists immediately before each chorus. The off-putting effect is unlikely to be the result of sloppy editing, as I doubt you'd make that blunder twice.

The chorus itself relays its simple concept in the abstract:

All the love, all the love
All the love you should've given
All the love, all the love
All the love we could've given

As an interesting development, verse three's seeming reference to music-making reveals a possible level of autobiography – perhaps Kate's most self-referential stanza ever:

The next time I dedicate
My life's work to the friends I make
I give them what they want to hear
They think I'm up to something weird
And up rears the head of fear in me

So now when they ring
I get my machine to let them in

To say 'I give them what they want to hear' doesn't sound like Kate Bush at all.

The penultimate section highlighting a succession of answerphone-message goodbyes was a fascinating and endearing touch. The explanation comes best from Kate's newsletter entry:

> One of the ideas for the song sparked when I came home from the studio late one night. I was using an answering machine to take the day's messages, and it had been going wrong a lot, gradually growing worse with time. It would speed peoples' voices up beyond recognition, and I just used to hope they would ring back again one day at normal speed. This particular night, I started to play back the tape, and the machine had neatly edited half a dozen messages together to leave 'Goodbye', 'See you', 'Cheers' and 'See you soon'. It was a strange thing to sit and listen to your friends ringing up, apparently just to say goodbye. I had several cassettes of peoples' messages, all ending with authentic farewells, and by copying them onto 1/4" tape and rearranging the order, we managed to synchronise the callers with the last verse of the song.

Editing would've been necessary, as the reality would've almost certainly been that after one message ended, she then heard the ending of the slightly longer one that came before it, and so on. In some cases, the words would've certainly cut in partway through (necessitating the editing), just like in the old cassette days when you might repeatedly reuse the same tape to record new albums onto, and if you listened until the end of a side, you'd hear the last moments of successive album endings. I'd wager that the machine suddenly 'editing' only the goodbyes together one after another would be absolutely impossible, as – after all – it was merely an analogue-tape answering machine, many of which at that time used microcassettes like those used in Dictaphones. The only variation those tapes/machines were capable of demonstrating were warbling, speeding up, slowing down, or absolutely just stopping dead.

## 'Houdini'

(Bush)
Released as a single B-side, 25 November 1983 (IRE), b/w 'Night Of The Swallow'
Personnel:
Kate Bush: vocals, piano, Fairlight
Stuart Elliott: drums
Eberhard Weber: electric upright bass
Dave Lawson, Andrew Powell: strings arrangement
Gordon Farrell: 'Houdini'
Del Palmer: 'Rosabel believe'

The idea for a song about famous Hungarian escapologist Harry Houdini had been on the table since the late stages of recording *Never For Ever.* The song 'Houdini' was to have the longest gestation of any on *The Dreaming* and kept being returned to throughout the album's recording. The lyric proved to be difficult to write in a general macro way as far as establishing and maintaining the right tone in order to do the story justice, right down to the details. One line, in particular, was as tricky a blighter to manifest from the ether as Harry's spirit had been for his wife Bess, when attempting to contact him via various mediums and spiritualists after his death. In the end, *both* worked, apparently. My guess would be that the difficult line was the ultimately fortifying 'Bound and drowned and paler than you've ever been', but it could've been any of them: the entire composition is so cohesive that no cracks show whatsoever.

Considering the attention shown to this recording over an extended period since its initial session at the Townhouse in the summer of 1981, the track came out as beautifully understated, arranged with not a note wasted over the piece's four stylistically individual repeating sections. The verses are carried by piano and bass (strings added in verse two), kick drum and bell-like Fairlight entering in the B sections. The C section's famously aggressive vocal is supported by piano, low growling Fairlight and that signature, pounding Townhouse drum sound.

Section D has the gorgeous surprise of a string quartet, arranged by Dave Lawson and Andrew Powell (producer and arranger of *The Kick Inside* and *Lionheart*). In the late 1960s, Powell had been a member of the English experimental rock group Henry Cow. Somehow, to think of someone from that group suddenly taking one of the most (if not *the* most) eccentric and bizarre songs ('Wuthering Heights') to the top of the charts globally, is mind-bending and exceptionally satisfying. The slightly dissonant string arrangement of 'Houdini' evokes the orchestral/chamber music of the early 20th century, with Eberhard Weber's melodic bass part interwoven, though still a feature. So subtle is the arrangement, the quartet plays in only three-part harmony for the first few bars.

Kate initially invited Weber to play by putting a call into a hotel he was staying at in Hamburg. When he arrived back from a rehearsal, the receptionist informed him of a call received from a Frau Busch in the UK. Calling back, Weber got no answer and was racking his brain over who the mystery caller might be. In the end, he received a letter in the mail when he got back home, and a trip to London for the session ensued. Kate told *The Guardian* that year: 'I realise how lucky I am. I realised making *The Dreaming* – when I was able to get Eberhard Weber to play on one track – that I was so lucky because people you like and respect will want to work with you.'

It's worth quoting the complimentary paragraph that Weber devoted to Bush in his 2015 autobiography *Eberhard Weber: A German Jazz Story*:

> Right from the start, I have found Kate to be a truly endearing person, warm-hearted, generous and humble. Even if I wanted to, I wouldn't be able to think of anything negative to say about her. My detractors will be shocked: Weber, the eternal critic, is full of praise! She reacted splendidly to my strokes of fate – my stroke in 2007 and the sudden, unexpected death of my wife Maja in 2011. An admirable, exceptional woman.

Unlike a piece like 'The Dreaming' – which had allowed for much artistic license and letting-down of the hair – communicating the plight of Harry and Bess Houdini in song demanded patience and subtlety. Kate explained at length in her newsletter:

> The side most people know of Houdini is that of the escapologist, but he spent many years of his life exposing mediums and seances as frauds. His mother had died, and in trying to make contact through such spiritual people, he realised how much pain was being inflicted on people already in sorrow – people who would part with money just for the chance of a few words from a past loved one. I feel he must've believed in the possibility of contact after death, and perhaps in his own way, by weeding out the frauds, he hoped to find just one that could not be proven to be a fake. He and his wife made a decision that if one of them should die and try to make contact, the other would know it was truly them through a code that only the two of them knew.

That code was 'Rosabelle, believe', which is sung in the track, and Del Palmer can be heard saying it (effected through an EQ filter). Visiting many mediums after Houdini's death, Bess eventually struck on a Mr. Ford, who said Harry was present and quoted the code back at Bess. This was verified in as much as it was reported in the newspapers. However, she later came to the conclusion that their code had been betrayed and she'd been tricked.

Kate continued:

> I was so aware of trying to do justice to the beauty of the subject and trying to understand what it must've been like to have been in love with such an extraordinary man and to have been loved by him. Singing the lead vocal was a matter of conjuring up that feeling again, and as the clock whirs and the song flashes back in time to when she watched him

> through the glass, he's on the other side underwater, and she hangs on to his every breath. We both wait.

This brings us to aspects of the story that Kate only discovered during the song's writing. She knew not that Houdini had even been married. In her words: 'His wife would often help him with his escapes. Before he was bound up and sealed away inside a tank or some dark box, she would give him a parting kiss, and as their lips met, she would pass him the key, which he would later use to unlock the padlocks that chained him'. This was, of course, famously conveyed in the sepia album cover image showing Kate and Del as the Houdini couple (taken by John Carder Bush and credited to his photography studio Kindlight), the album artwork elsewhere isolating the lyric line, 'With a kiss I'd pass the key'.

What ended up being Houdini's last trick was scuppered by the need to smash a water tank to free him. But what led to his death occurred in a Montreal dressing room in 1926 after he told one Jocelyn Whitehead that he could withstand stomach punches, after which she surprised him with several violent blows. Developing peritonitis, Houdini died in Detroit nine days later at Halloween.

In the lyric, the story is disseminated in the verses via Bess seeking Harry at seances and in the B and C sections back in time at the escape events:

> (Verse 1)
> I wait at the table
> And hold hands with weeping strangers
> Wait for you to join the group
> The tambourine jingle-jangle
> The medium roams and rambles
> Not taken in, I break the circle
> I want this man to go away now
> (B1)
> With a kiss I'd pass the key
> And feel your tongue teasing and receiving

(C1)
With your spit still on my lip
You hit the water

The piece ends peacefully and entirely appropriately, being on the 6 chord of the minor key.

## 'Get Out Of My House'

(Bush)
Personnel:
Kate Bush: vocals, piano, Fairlight
Preston Hayman: drums
Jimmy Bain: bass
Alan Murphy: guitar
Paddy Bush: backing vocals
Paul Hardiman: 'Eeyore'
Esmail Sheikh: drum talk

The fact that the closing track is titled 'Get Out Of My House' should preclude it from having to be at the end: it's just a bit too obvious. Plus, the raised energy of the track feels like it would work much better closer to the beginning of the album – perhaps as the second song, making it a one-two punch with 'Sat In Your Lap'. But in defence of 'Get Out Of My House', its percussive vitality does offer respite and levity after the 13 minutes of solemnity that come immediately before it, though it seems to me that 'Night Of The Swallow' would've made a beautiful and impressive album closer.

Originally, the idea was for the album to be more rhythmic anyway – 'Sat In Your Lap', 'Leave It Open' and 'Get Out Of My House' being the first tracks worked on, with Hugh Padgham. Kate was inspired by the 1977 Stephen King novel *The Shining* and the 1979 Ridley Scott science-fiction movie *Alien,* which both involved characters in isolation at the mercy of some unseen presence – psychological and perhaps ghostly in the former and absolutely physical in the latter. The necessity-versus-uncertainty of every move is reflected in the comfort and forward-motion of Alan Murphy's ringing guitar introduction and the pummelling drums' angular, choppy, but repetitive and infectious rhythms.

But sitting astride is the song's serious side. The lyric superficially appears to be a haunted house story, though it is, in fact, a metaphor for a human who has been hurt and won't let anybody in. Placed at the front door is a metaphorical concierge played by Paddy Bush:

I am the concierge *chez-moi*, honey
Won't letcha in for love nor money
My home, my joy
I'm barred and bolted and I

Somehow, the intruder gets in and approaches the room the subject is hiding in. Both then become shape-shifters, the subject turning into a bird, eventually turning to face the intruder with no recourse left but to scream or let out the donkey 'Eeyore!'s that provide yet another distinguishing feature. These particular vocal details – the humourous idea of engineer Paul Hardiman – were inspired by the 'Star Turn On 45 (Pints)' records that were getting airplay in England at the time, though they largely failed to chart, being parodies of the Stars On 45 medleys that *were* consuming the world's singles charts at the time. You've *got* to give Kate and crew credit for allowing the final track to project such unpretentious levity in the face of – or maybe in spite of – the serious content elsewhere on *The Dreaming*. Perhaps the track *does* belong at the end *after* all.

'Get Out Of My House' was apparently a beast to record and kept changing over time, becoming virtually twice its original length – something that had never happened with a Kate recording before. Also unique for a Kate Bush record up to this point was the song virtually being a duet towards the end, though not much attention has been given to that fact. Back in the 1980s, when I first heard the album, I barely even noticed the voice of Paul Hardiman, though that could've been due to his vocal having a lot of low mids and being slightly buried in the mix. But his contribution was substantial, singing the following lines:

Woman let me in
Let me bring in the memories
Woman let me in
Let me bring in the Devil dreams

Woman let me in
I turn into the wind

I blow you a cold kiss
Stronger than the song's hit

There's a lot to take in with so much going on, and it's my understanding that this track took a full week to mix.

## B-Sides

### **'Lord Of The Reedy River'** (Leitch)

Released as a single B-side, 19 June 1981 (UK), b/w 'Sat In Your Lap'
Personnel:
Kate Bush: vocals, Fairlight
Unidentified: male voice

Welsh folk-pop singer Mary Hopkin was the first to release this gorgeous Donovan song, opening her Paul McCartney-produced 1969 debut album *Post Card* with it, though Donovan *was* the accompanist on that recording. He exposed the song again a few months later, performing a solo version in a scene from director Mel Stuart's 1969 American romantic-comedy movie *If It's Tuesday, This Must Be Belgium.* (The presence of an electric guitar overdub – if not added afterwards – would suggest the performance was mimed in the movie.) In that film, the song's intrinsic beauty was more to the fore, as it seemed more urgent coming from a male, even though Hopkin *had* retained the lyric's male perspective. Around this time, Donovan recorded the song again for his 1969 American-only album, *Barabajagal,* though the track didn't make it to the final cut. Released in 2005 on that album's extended edition, the song's original omission is now easy to explain, being that its jazz-combo arrangement was not only out of step with the tone of the album but the busy arrangement also clearly ran roughshod over the delicate song, rendering the surface almost ugly in parts (not to mention seeming unnecessarily long, even at its mere three minutes). But humbly buried away on side four of Donovan's double 1971 album *HMS Donovan* was what I'd consider to be the song's quintessential rendition. Playing the song in a lower key there gave the piece an even richer depth, only made more profound through the title line having a measure of 9/8 to trip you up as if actually wading through a reedy river. But it doesn't do it every single time – the reality would indeed be that some steps are easier to take than others: a fantastic, subtle example of prosody.

Kate made the composition entirely her own, using pan-pipe samples instead of acoustic guitar. Sadly, she also dispensed with the 9/8 idea completely, sticking to the original 4/4 rhythm. Although, with no basic leading percussion instrument evident besides the samples and their occasional digital delay, the whole thing seems to just float anyway and doesn't feel rigid tempo-wise at all. She also changed the pronoun perspective from 'she' to 'I', which was perhaps a misstep considering the narrator's gender is imbued in the song title. But, with the word 'Lord' not being uttered even once in the song, Kate could've gotten away with titling it 'Lady Of The Reedy River', and it would've worked – though, the word 'Lord' could also work merely as a metaphor.

Small additional sounds are tastefully incorporated, providing detail but not detracting from the main focus: that voice. These sounds consist of an occasional unidentified scratching noise suggesting the creaking of a dinghy, a reverb-smothered male voice saying 'reedy river', laughter and Kate's amassed choral voices towards the end: an arrangement technique that, in her hands, has always been stirring. Conspicuous in their presence are Fairlight vocal samples sounding virtually identical to the ones heard in the choirboy sections of 'All The Love'. More impressive are the real water drops and natural room reverberation on the vocal – a consequence of it being recorded down at the Townhouse' unused basement swimming pool, as Kate wanted to sound as if she was floating along a river. This is a fine example of the kind of method technique that she took to an extreme years later when filming a video for a new recording of the *Hounds Of Love* song 'And Dream Of Sheep', immersed in freezing water while simultaneously singing. (This video was projected onto a screen at the *Before The Dawn* concerts in 2014.)

They went to a lot of trouble for a recording that was absolutely intended as a B-side – one of the first things recorded with Nick Launay at the Townhouse for the flipside of the 'Sat In Your Lap' single, released quickly, more than a year in advance of the album. Even so, the recording of this

B-side was treated with great care and can hardly be thought of as a throwaway. The 7" picture sleeve included the note, 'Thanks to Donovan for writing such a beautiful song', and the B-side runout groove was etched with the words, 'THANK YOU DONOVAN'.

**'Dreamtime (Instrumental Version)'** (Bush)
Released as a single B-side, 19 June 1981 (UK), b/w 'Sat In Your Lap'
Released as a single B-side, 1982, b/w 'Suspended In Gaffa' (FRA)
Personnel:
Kate Bush: vocals, piano, Fairlight
Stuart Elliott: drums
Rolf Harris: didjeridu
Percy Edwards: animals
Paddy Bush: bullroarer, backing vocals
Gosfield Goers: crowd
This is basically an instrumental version of 'The Dreaming' with certain mix changes, but a complete remix from scratch would not have been necessary. However, certain elements were able to be accentuated due to them not stepping on the lead vocal. This mix includes many but not all of the backing vocals – depending on what you consider to be a backing vocal here or actually important to the melodic framework. But it could just *seem* like certain things are louder thanks to the absent lead vocal. It really sounds like not much was altered at all, the opportunity for change really being in the eight bars of instrumental between what would be the choruses and their following verses, where there's an added Kate vocal track (absent from the album version) singing 'dreamtime'. But my guess would be that *that* vocal was recorded back when the song was called 'Dreamtime', was considered superfluous after the retitling, but nevertheless found an unexpected home in this mix.

Much trouble was taken for this B-side, rather than just running off a straight instrumental mix minus vocal, which would've been the easiest and least labour-intensive thing to do. It begins with several beats of didjeridu getting started, three bars with tom-toms and then the entry of kick drum at bar four, which is where the album version began. After the new vocal's entry at 0:59, you can clearly hear the aptly-named 'Gosfield Goers' at 3:10 yelling the phrase, 'Find 'em in the raw', followed by, 'In the raw', and – at 3:25 – the long crowd yell extended through Fairlight looping and a long reverb effect.

This mix is one minute and 18 seconds longer than the album version, having an extra ten seconds at the beginning and an extra one minute and eight seconds at the end, running longer than the album version's original length of 4:13. At the very end, Rolf Harris stops playing the didjeridu and utters, 'And stuff like that'.

**'Ne T'en Fui Pas'** (Bush, Chandler, Jeaneau)
Released as a single B-side, 29 October 1982 (UK), b/w 'There Goes A Tenner'
Released as a single B-side, 1982 (GER/NE/SPA), b/w 'Suspended In Gaffa'
Released as a single B-side, January 1983 (AUS), b/w 'Suspended In Gaffa'
Released as a single A-side as 'Ne T'enfuis Pas', July 1983 (CAN), b/w 'Dreamtime'
Released as a single A-side as 'Ne T'enfuis Pas (Remix)', July 1983 (FRA), b/w 'Un Baiser D'Enfant'
Personnel:
Kate Bush: vocals, piano, Fairlight
Del Palmer: LinnDrum programming, fretless bass

The highlight of this recording is Del Palmer's fluid fretless bass playing, which is a feature, not that the LinnDrum doesn't first catch your attention. The keyboard sound is mainly Fairlight organ, with some piano buried in there later on. The lyric being sung entirely in French doesn't stop that rich Kate Bush emotion from coming through. Knowing that the woman in the song is fearful her lover might leave her isn't necessary – it's still obvious that this is heavy business, the English title being 'Don't Run Away' or 'Don't Fly Away'.

The French A-side single was a slight remix with a louder vocal and was the version that appeared in the 1990 Kate Bush box set *This Woman's Work: Anthology 1978-1990.*

The translation came partly from French actress Vivienne Chandler, who'd appeared in Stanley Kubrick's *A Clockwork Orange* (1971). She was also a photographer and contributed to the design of *The Dreaming, Hounds Of Love* (1985) and the Kate Bush compilation, *The Whole Story* (1986). Having two children with Kate's brother, John Carder Bush, Vivienne at one point went under the professional name Holly Bush.

**'Un Baiser D'Enfant (The Infant Kiss)'** (Bush)

Released as a single A-side, 1983 (CAN), b/w 'Suspended In Gaffa'
Released as a single B-side, July 1983 (FRA), b/w 'Ne T'enfuis Pas (Remix)'
Personnel:
Kate Bush: vocals, piano
Alan Murphy: guitar
Adam Sceaping: viol
Joseph Sceaping: Lironi

This *Never For Ever* deep cut is here sung in French, but the backing track is identical to that on the album. The only other changes are to some melody notes to better suit the new pronunciation. Though the backing vocals are largely wordless, the words 'gets too much' remain at the end of verse two, simultaneous to the new French lead vocal singing 'soit trop tard' right over the top of them. The lead vocal itself emanates more depth of character than the timid and almost innocent English vocal had.

The held closing chord lasts a full nine seconds – five seconds longer than on *Never For Ever* due to its following track, 'Night Scented Stock', cross-fading in.

Unfortunately, this beautiful song has received some flak in recent years, largely due to poorly-researched critics letting their imaginations run wild over lines like 'I've never fallen for a little boy before' and 'What is this infant kiss that sends my body tingling?'. The lyric was – after all – just a giant metaphor and re-imagining of ideas from the Henry James novel *The Turn Of The Screw,* filtered through its 1961 movie version, *The Innocents.* This song is as innocent as its title suggests. 'The Infant Kiss' – is it a kiss *from* an infant or *for* an infant? And either way, what does the phrase say about the *quality* of the kiss? Nothing. I could go on. If Frank Zappa can win a 1971 court case defending at analytical length the lyrics of songs with much more suggestive titles, and if a recent surge in legislation where acts like The Restoring Artistic Protection Act can affirm that 'Every single artist, no matter the discipline, should be able to express themselves without fear of prosecution', I doubt someone like Kate Bush has anything to worry about.

As recently as 2019, the 'Ne T'en Fui Pas' single was re-released as a 12" vinyl promo for Kate's *The Other Sides* compilation, retaining the diabolical 'Un Baiser D'Enfant' as its B-side, not to mention the song's inclusion on the album.

# Afterwards

In late May 1982, Kate attempted to take a break in Jamaica but was as restless as she'd been while recording the album when sleep had been a rarity. Clearly in workaholic mode, she couldn't deal with the sudden shift from a tiny, windowless studio to a paradise where even the sound of birds singing was an irritation. So she returned to London.

*The Dreaming* had been mastered at EMI America by Ron McMaster (who *really* sounds like the guy you'd want to do it!), and Kate prepared for intense album promotion. But first, in July – with 48 hours' notice – came an invite to replace David Bowie in a single-song performance at the Royal Rock Gala in aid of The Prince's Trust before HRH The Prince of Wales. Taking place at London's Dominion Theatre, the song selected was – of all things – the *Never For Ever* song 'The Wedding List' (less impactful and interesting being dropped down two keys for some reason). Despite the lack of a better song, the band lineup was sensational! – Phil Collins (Genesis) on drums, Mick Karn (Japan) on fretless bass, Gary Brooker (Procol Harum) on electric piano, Dave Formula (Magazine, Visage) on synth, Peter Hope-Evans (Medicine Head) on harmonica and Pete Townshend (The Who) and Midge Ure (Ultravox) on guitars. (Incidentally, in 1972 – one year before Pink Floyd's initially-gold-selling stylus ruiner – Medicine Head released an album titled *Dark Side Of The Moon*!)

To view this live performance is a real lesson in professionalism. Not one of the all-star band tried to steal attention from Kate (or whoever was out front that night – Robert Plant was next), and even *she* clearly had no tickets on herself, appearing as if she was a kindergarten teacher who'd come straight from work – although, bassist Mick Karn *was* difficult to ignore, planted there like some retro-futurist android. (The video for 'The Dreaming' had probably not aired yet, otherwise, Pete Townshend could've worn a white boilersuit in tribute!) The band all took great care with the song and didn't just throw it away – though, to be fair, the tempo changes would've required a level of rehearsal. Pete Townshend's playing was particularly impressive, demonstrating a clean, subdued, more contemporary rhythm sound quite different from what we might've expected from him. One can only imagine what *The Dreaming* could've sounded like had this been the band that played on it. It would've really been something. But, of course, the album was about the material and what was in Kate Bush's head. It was a cerebral record, and sometimes, if you put clever songs up against too much instrumental virtuosity (not that the album's players weren't virtuosos), the two things can vie for attention, and you can end up with a homogenous lump of something that sounds unfinished, its potential having failed to be adequately chiselled from the rock: certainly in the hands of a first-time producer, as Kate was in this instance. Considering that, the criticism levelled at her for taking on the production task falls flat, as – despite what some might think of the album – she certainly avoided the above-mentioned clash of clever writing meets clever playing. No easy task – but she got the balance right.

Now is where the art-meets-commerce cliche comes in. The album was being described as Bush's least accessible, though *she* referred to it as her 'most emotional'. She told *The Guardian* that year: 'To me, the best music has always been that which gives you tingles up and down the spine, and that's what I try and create. It seems to me the only way you can do that is to really establish a mood, as if you were making a film – concentrate on the emotional charges that are coming from a person or situation, and try to capture them on record'.

She elaborated to *ZigZag* in 1982:

> I don't know how they're going to take it. I think the people who've understood where I've been so far are going to be into it. They're expecting something different each time, so it's almost predictable in that respect. But I think a lot of people won't like it. They probably won't understand what it's about. I find the more I write the stuff, the less I worry about this and the better it is. I remember that on the second and third albums, there were lots of times when I was writing

> a song, and I kept thinking about what people were going to think of it. I'd rather not do that and lose some of the people who are into my music because I'm really doing what I want to do. I'm going where I want, and I'm going to keep going for it. I've no idea what's going to happen.

Promoting the album was a real battle, but Kate was bullheaded. She had to be: 'Everyone says it is the least commercial album ever, and it's true. It worries me a little, but it's the way I want to go, so I'm happy about that'.

EMI Records were reluctant, feeling the record didn't have a single: another cliche. 'The Dreaming' was at least fun, if not directly accessible. But Kate was fine with that: to write another radio hit had not been a goal. But it's interesting that the single failed, considering 1982 was slap-bang in the middle of perhaps the most adventurous time in pop music when the public were at their most open-minded and accepting – musicians were expecting a lot of listeners, and listeners were responding. But a record couldn't promote itself, and certainly not without airplay.

Thankfully, Kate had a stalwart believer in EMI's new A&R and marketing head, David Munns, who'd left the company in 1979 but was now back. It was he who gave *The Dreaming* the green light, but he fell short of putting much weight behind the promotion. It was up to Kate to bust her gut, which she did, trekking around the UK and the continent to talk about the record on almost any show that would have her – meaning, she didn't see any outlet as being beneath her. And it's not like they didn't reciprocate – everyone still wanted to talk to her, and her personal profile was still high.

In the TV appearances that included a performance, she lip-synched while executing the choreography of the videos – sometimes alone – with the exception of 'There Goes A Tenner', which had little-to-no choreography in the video but *was* given a full three-dancer routine for the appearance in Newcastle on the music show *Razmatazz*. By this time, this was the closest thing you could get to a Kate Bush concert. But better than a concert, some of these performances happened down on the floor with audience members sitting just feet away. This was the case with one appearance in France where she mimed 'Suspended In Gaffa', and indeed for the same song on the German show *Bananas,* though *there* she was ogled by a large group of hanging puppets who I'd guess didn't quite appreciate the proximity!

Appearing on the Munich TV show *Na Sowas!,* Kate and two male companions undertook the dance routine for 'The Dreaming', all wearing their costumes from the video. It's uncertain whether she'd absconded from London with the actual outfit she'd worn in the film, which could've been risky should the popular boilersuit-with-accoutrements have been required for yet another rock video by someone or other. Afterwards, host Thomas Gottschalk presented Kate with a gold record for *Never For Ever:* such was the respect she still commanded.

Kate Bush could also still move a unit or two. *The Dreaming* entered the UK album chart at number three – its peak – spending only 12 weeks in the chart. Compare that to *Never For Ever,* which had entered at number one for one week but remained in the chart for only another 22 weeks. *The Dreaming* – though selling only 60,000 in its initial run – still charted higher than the bigger-selling *Lionheart* (300,000), which had only reached six. Which is really the bigger success? I guess it's a matter of what you *call* success and what you're listening for. When it comes to music, statistics don't count for much. There's no denying the hook-laden directness of the two big (ish) *Lionheart* singles, 'Wow' (14) and 'Hammer Horror' (44). Both are musically brilliant, overtly theatrical, extremely listenable and were widely popular (at the time) despite the latter's gimmicky approach (distasteful to some), and the former being a surprising, scathing and matter-of-fact indictment of show-business machinations whether you wanted to hear about them or not. Yet, 'Wow' still peaked a full 30 notches higher than its album mate with its more obviously accessible subject matter. You can probably put the success of 'Wow' down purely to its extended and repetitive 'wow-wow-

wow' hook with squeaky karate *kiai* at the end (Kate was a karate advocate). The public have always been easily reeled in with gimmicks like that. If she'd done that squeal in 'Hammer Horror' instead, it may have been the bigger hit. Harsh, perhaps, but this is all to make the point about the futility of judging musical success by statistics. Does an initial 60,000 in sales make *The Dreaming* the inferior album? No, it doesn't – the album existed before its sales statistics did; therefore, it already had intrinsic, objective worth. Had it been her debut, it still would've been praised and might one day have been held in some kind of esteem equal to how *The Kick Inside* has been. But, such a scenario might've caused Kate to attempt music that was more commercial afterwards: a reversal of the reality. Therefore, *The Dreaming* would be the one they all talk about now – *'Remember that fabulous arty debut that was followed up with all that poppy stuff?'*. This *could've* happened, and it *has* happened to others. Within this whole idea dwells the fundamental, mercurial whimsy of record executives, critics, consumers and sales – all ultimately unmeasurable as a unit and therefore unreliable when it comes to determining an album's true merit when held up against its competitors.

Speaking of executives, just four short years after Kate first became the darling of EMI, certain company staffers even stooped as low as to criticise her latest move right to her face. Accusing her of not providing any obvious singles, she matter-of-factly responded, 'That's right. I didn't write any.'

Certain factions of the press didn't help either. One *Daily Mail* example stated that – during the making of the record – Kate had virtually doubled in weight. This was, of course, patently untrue, borne out by the elfin creature seen treading the boards in the promotional tour of 1982. That laborious promotional grind came to an end in November; Kate came off the road and disappeared into effective reclusive splendour. But, waiting in the wings was some sweet vindication in the form of *The Dreaming* reaching the top 200 in the USA and being picked up by college radio there. It wasn't Kate but her *audience* that was expanding.

## Coda

It took six months for Kate to recover from making *The Dreaming*. Her doctor told her to take time off after diagnosing her as suffering from nervous exhaustion and stress. Thus, she became the invisible woman, soon setting up a recording studio on the old family farm in Kent and beginning work on what was to become *Hounds Of Love*. That album was completed in the early summer of 1985, which, in theory, meant that Kate could've had time to prepare for a possible Live Aid appearance. But an invite never came despite Bob Geldof being a big fan and despite Kate having appeared in the Royal Rock Gala, which, in effect, had been like a little practice run for events like Live Aid. I'd guess Kate being long off the gigging treadmill could've had a lot to do with it. But, she *is* known to have said she might've reciprocated had she been asked.

Kate Bush was, of course, still popular, and perhaps her most successful period was still to come, with her number one album *Hounds Of Love* and its four top 40 singles. But perhaps the depth of hers or anyone's personal popularity can also be measured by a capacity for attracting *unwanted* attention. In 1993, *Time Out* journalist Nick Coleman wrote of a friend named Catherine who apparently was living in the attic of Kate's childhood home in Kent. Catherine would sometimes get mail for Kate Bush, which was never opened. But one letter came addressed only to 'Catherine'. Opening it, it contained psycho-nonsense about how the writer was *watching* 'Catherine'. Letters continued to arrive, apparently from the same source, and increasingly disturbing. On the day she decided to go to the police, a letter arrived referring to her 'poetry and music', this time including the name 'Kate'. Mail for Kate Bush continued to arrive and remained unopened. But one day, a letter arrived addressed to Catherine Earnshaw – from a Harley Street doctor, saying Catherine was in good health. Catherine decided to forward this to Kate Bush's record company before she realised Catherine Earnshaw was the name of the heroine from the Emily Bronte novel *Wuthering Heights*. It seems all the disturbing mail had come from some character with an obsession that combined the fictional character and the real Kate Bush into one praiseworthy entity – the realisation of which I'd imagine would've been quite a relief for Catherine with a C. Apparently, she continued to be quite haunted by this, especially on stormy nights when the wind would cause the attic window casement to creak, and she'd imagine a Kate or Kathy of some description outside calling to be let in. Cab drivers constantly telling Catherine, 'That's where Kate Bush used to live', probably didn't help either.

It's fascinating imagery, especially when you remember that *Hounds Of Love* was largely recorded on that property. Kate Bush's artistic work was nothing if not fun, and admirers of it know not to get too wound up in the seriousness of it all. But if you let your imagination run wild, you can see Kathy, Kate, the hounds, Harry and Bess – even those *boilersuits* – and maybe even some sort of Hammer-esque horror all coming at you in some kind of dreaming.

# Bibliography

Irwin, C., Kate Bush: Paranoia and Passion of the Kate Inside (*Melody Maker,* 4 October 1980)

Brown, M., Kate Bush: Kate Takes Charge (*The Guardian,* 11 September 1982)

Needs, K., Kate Bush: Dream Time in the Bush (*ZigZag,* November 1982)

Zappa, F., Occhiogrosso, P., *The Real Frank Zappa Book* (Simon & Schuster, 1989)

Sutcliffe, P., Iron Maiden: Kate Bush (*Q,* November 1989)

Coleman, N., Kate Bush: Daft as a Bush (*Time Out,* November 1993)

Maconie, S., Kate Bush: Little Miss Can't Be Wrong (*Q,* December 1993)

Ivashkin, A., *Alfred Schnittke* (Phaidon Press, 1996)

Thomson, G., *Under The Ivy: The Life And Music Of Kate Bush* (Omnibus Press, 2010)

Lynskey, D., Kate Bush: The Mystery Dance (*The Word,* December 2011)

Weber, E., *Eberhard Weber: A German Jazz Story* (Sagas, 2015)

Rouhani, N., Federal Bill Limiting Use of Rap Lyrics in Court Reintroduced in Congress (*Billboard,* 27 April 2023)

## Websites

*gaffa.org*

*katebushencyclopedia.com*

*UKRockHistory (YouTube)*

*uncut.co.uk*

**On Track Series**

AC/DC – Chris Sutton 978-1-78952-307-2
Allman Brothers Band – Andrew Wild 978-1-78952-252-5
Tori Amos – Lisa Torem 978-1-78952-142-9
Aphex Twin – Beau Waddell 978-1-78952-267-9
Asia – Peter Braidis 978-1-78952-099-6
Badfinger – Robert Day-Webb 978-1-878952-176-4
Barclay James Harvest – Keith and Monica Domone 978-1-78952-067-5
Beck – Arthur Lizie 978-1-78952-258-7
The Beat, General Public, Fine Young Cannibals – Steve Parry 978-1-78952-274-7
The Beatles – Andrew Wild 978-1-78952-009-5
The Beatles Solo 1969-1980 – Andrew Wild 978-1-78952-030-9
Blue Oyster Cult – Jacob Holm-Lupo 978-1-78952-007-1
Blur – Matt Bishop 978-178952-164-1
Marc Bolan and T.Rex – Peter Gallagher 978-1-78952-124-5
Kate Bush – Bill Thomas 978-1-78952-097-2
The Byrds – Andy McArthur 978-1-78952-280-8
Camel – Hamish Kuzminski 978-1-78952-040-8
Captain Beefheart – Opher Goodwin 978-1-78952-235-8
Caravan – Andy Boot 978-1-78952-127-6
Cardiacs – Eric Benac 978-1-78952-131-3
Wendy Carlos – Mark Marrington 978-1-78952-331-7
The Carpenters – Paul Tornbohm 978-1-78952-301-0
Nick Cave and The Bad Seeds – Dominic Sanderson 978-1-78952-240-2
Eric Clapton Solo – Andrew Wild 978-1-78952-141-2
The Clash – Nick Assirati 978-1-78952-077-4
Elvis Costello and The Attractions – Georg Purvis 978-1-78952-129-0
Crosby, Stills and Nash – Andrew Wild 978-1-78952-039-2
Creedence Clearwater Revival – Tony Thompson 978-178952-237-2
The Damned – Morgan Brown 978-1-78952-136-8
David Bowie 1964 to 1982 – Carl Ewens 978-1-78952-324-9
Deep Purple and Rainbow 1968-79 – Steve Pilkington 978-1-78952-002-6
Depeche Mode – Brian J. Robb 978-1-78952-277-8
Dire Straits – Andrew Wild 978-1-78952-044-6
The Divine Comedy – Alan Draper 978-1-78952-308-9
The Doors – Tony Thompson 978-1-78952-137-5
Dream Theater – Jordan Blum 978-1-78952-050-7
Bob Dylan 1962-1970 – Opher Goodwin 978-1-78952-275-2
Eagles – John Van der Kiste 978-1-78952-260-0
Earth, Wind and Fire – Bud Wilkins 978-1-78952-272-3
Electric Light Orchestra – Barry Delve 978-1-78952-152-8
Emerson Lake and Palmer – Mike Goode 978-1-78952-000-2
Fairport Convention – Kevan Furbank 978-1-78952-051-4
Peter Gabriel – Graeme Scarfe 978-1-78952-138-2
Genesis – Stuart MacFarlane 978-1-78952-005-7
Gentle Giant – Gary Steel 978-1-78952-058-3
Gong – Kevan Furbank 978-1-78952-082-8
Green Day – William E. Spevack 978-1-78952-261-7

Steve Hackett – Geoffrey Feakes 978-1-78952-098-9
Hall and Oates – Ian Abrahams 978-1-78952-167-2
Peter Hammill – Richard Rees Jones 978-1-78952-163-4
Roy Harper – Opher Goodwin 978-1-78952-130-6
Hawkwind (new edition) – Duncan Harris 978-1-78952-290-7
Jimi Hendrix – Emma Stott 978-1-78952-175-7
The Hollies – Andrew Darlington 978-1-78952-159-7
Horslips – Richard James 978-1-78952-263-1
The Human League and The Sheffield Scene –
Andrew Darlington 978-1-78952-186-3
Humble Pie –Robert Day-Webb 978-1-78952-2761
Ian Hunter – G. Mick Smith 978-1-78952-304-1
The Incredible String Band – Tim Moon 978-1-78952-107-8
INXS – Manny Grillo 978-1-78952-302-7
Iron Maiden – Steve Pilkington 978-1-78952-061-3
Joe Jackson – Richard James 978-1-78952-189-4
The Jam – Stan Jeffries 978-1-78952-299-0
Jefferson Airplane – Richard Butterworth 978-1-78952-143-6
Jethro Tull – Jordan Blum 978-1-78952-016-3
Elton John in the 1970s – Peter Kearns 978-1-78952-034-7
Billy Joel – Lisa Torem 978-1-78952-183-2
Judas Priest – John Tucker 978-1-78952-018-7
Kansas – Kevin Cummings 978-1-78952-057-6
Killing Joke – Nic Ransome 978-1-78952-273-0
The Kinks – Martin Hutchinson 978-1-78952-172-6
Korn – Matt Karpe 978-1-78952-153-5
Led Zeppelin – Steve Pilkington 978-1-78952-151-1
Level 42 – Matt Philips 978-1-78952-102-3
Little Feat – Georg Purvis – 978-1-78952-168-9
Magnum – Matthew Taylor – 978-1-78952-286-0
Aimee Mann – Jez Rowden 978-1-78952-036-1
Ralph McTell – Paul O. Jenkins 978-1-78952-294-5
Metallica – Barry Wood 978-1-78952-269-3
Joni Mitchell – Peter Kearns 978-1-78952-081-1
The Moody Blues – Geoffrey Feakes 978-1-78952-042-2
Motorhead – Duncan Harris 978-1-78952-173-3
Nektar – Scott Meze – 978-1-78952-257-0
New Order – Dennis Remmer – 978-1-78952-249-5
Nightwish – Simon McMurdo – 978-1-78952-270-9
Nirvana – William E. Spevack 978-1-78952-318-8
Laura Nyro – Philip Ward 978-1-78952-182-5
Oasis – 978-1-78952-300-3
Mike Oldfield – Ryan Yard 978-1-78952-060-6
Opeth – Jordan Blum 978-1-78-952-166-5
Pearl Jam – Ben L. Connor 978-1-78952-188-7
Tom Petty – Richard James 978-1-78952-128-3
Pink Floyd – Richard Butterworth 978-1-78952-242-6
The Police – Pete Braidis 978-1-78952-158-0

Porcupine Tree – Nick Holmes 978-1-78952-144-3
Procol Harum – Scott Meze 978-1-78952-315-7
Queen – Andrew Wild 978-1-78952-003-3
Radiohead – William Allen 978-1-78952-149-8
Rancid – Paul Matts 978-1-78952-187-0
Lou Reed 1972-1986 – Ethan Roy 978-1-78952-283-9
Renaissance – David Detmer 978-1-78952-062-0
REO Speedwagon – Jim Romag 978-1-78952-262-4
The Rolling Stones 1963-80 – Steve Pilkington 978-1-78952-017-0
Linda Ronstadt 1969-1989 – Daryl O. Lawrence 987-1-78952-293-8
Sensational Alex Harvey Band – Peter Gallagher 978-1-7952-289-1
The Small Faces and The Faces – Andrew Darlington 978-1-78952-316-4
The Smashing Pumpkins – Matt Karpe 978-1-7952-291-4
The Smiths and Morrissey – Tommy Gunnarsson 978-1-78952-140-5
Spirit – Rev. Keith A. Gordon – 978-1-78952- 248-8
Soft Machine – Scott Meze 978-1078952-271-6
Stackridge – Alan Draper 978-1-78952-232-7
Status Quo the Frantic Four Years – Richard James 978-1-78952-160-3
Steely Dan – Jez Rowden 978-1-78952-043-9
The Stranglers – Martin Hutchinson 978-1-78952-323-2
Talk Talk – Gary Steel 978-1-78952-284-6
Tears For Fears – Paul Clark – 978-178952-238-9
Thin Lizzy – Graeme Stroud 978-1-78952-064-4
Tool – Matt Karpe 978-1-78952-234-1
Toto – Jacob Holm-Lupo 978-1-78952-019-4
U2 – Eoghan Lyng 978-1-78952-078-1
UFO – Richard James 978-1-78952-073-6
Ultravox – Brian J. Robb 978-1-78952-330-0
Van Der Graaf Generator – Dan Coffey 978-1-78952-031-6
Van Halen – Morgan Brown – 9781-78952-256-3
Suzanne Vega – Lisa Torem 978-1-78952-281-5
Jack White And The White Stripes – Ben L. Connor 978-1-78952-303-4
The Who – Geoffrey Feakes 978-1-78952-076-7
Roy Wood and the Move – James R Turner 978-1-78952-008-8
Yes (new edition) – Stephen Lambe 978-1-78952-282-2
Neil Young 1963 to 1970 – Oper Goodwin 978-1-78952-298-3
Frank Zappa 1966 to 1979 – Eric Benac 978-1-78952-033-0
Warren Zevon – Peter Gallagher 978-1-78952-170-2
The Zombies – Emma Stott 978-1-78952-297-6
10CC – Peter Kearns 978-1-78952-054-5

**Decades Series**
The Bee Gees in the 1960s – Andrew Mon Hughes et al 978-1-78952-148-1
The Bee Gees in the 1970s – Andrew Mon Hughes et al 978-1-78952-179-5
Black Sabbath in the 1970s – Chris Sutton 978-1-78952-171-9
Britpop – Peter Richard Adams and Matt Pooler 978-1-78952-169-6
Phil Collins in the 1980s – Andrew Wild 978-1-78952-185-6
Alice Cooper in the 1970s – Chris Sutton 978-1-78952-104-7

Alice Cooper in the 1980s – Chris Sutton 978-1-78952-259-4
Curved Air in the 1970s – Laura Shenton 978-1-78952-069-9
Donovan in the 1960s – Jeff Fitzgerald 978-1-78952-233-4
Bob Dylan in the 1980s – Don Klees 978-1-78952-157-3
Brian Eno in the 1970s – Gary Parsons 978-1-78952-239-6
Faith No More in the 1990s – Matt Karpe 978-1-78952-250-1
Fleetwood Mac in the 1970s – Andrew Wild 978-1-78952-105-4
Fleetwood Mac in the 1980s – Don Klees 978-178952-254-9
Focus in the 1970s – Stephen Lambe 978-1-78952-079-8
Free and Bad Company in the 1970s – John Van der Kiste 978-1-78952-178-8
Genesis in the 1970s – Bill Thomas 978178952-146-7
George Harrison in the 1970s – Eoghan Lyng 978-1-78952-174-0
Kiss in the 1970s – Peter Gallagher 978-1-78952-246-4
Manfred Mann's Earth Band in the 1970s – John Van der Kiste 978178952-243-3
Marillion in the 1980s – Nathaniel Webb 978-1-78952-065-1
Van Morrison in the 1970s – Peter Childs – 978-1-78952-241-9
Mott the Hoople & Ian Hunter in the 1970s – John Van der Kiste 978-1-78-952-162-7
Pink Floyd In The 1970s – Georg Purvis 978-1-78952-072-9
Suzi Quatro in the 1970s – Darren Johnson 978-1-78952-236-5
Queen in the 1970s – James Griffiths 978-1-78952-265-5
Roxy Music in the 1970s – Dave Thompson 978-1-78952-180-1
Slade in the 1970s – Darren Johnson 978-1-78952-268-6
Status Quo in the 1980s – Greg Harper 978-1-78952-244-0
Tangerine Dream in the 1970s – Stephen Palmer 978-1-78952-161-0
The Sweet in the 1970s – Darren Johnson 978-1-78952-139-9
Uriah Heep in the 1970s – Steve Pilkington 978-1-78952-103-0
Van der Graaf Generator in the 1970s – Steve Pilkington 978-1-78952-245-7
Rick Wakeman in the 1970s – Geoffrey Feakes 978-1-78952-264-8
Yes in the 1980s – Stephen Lambe with David Watkinson 978-1-78952-125-2

**Rock Classics Series**
90125 by Yes – Stephen Lambe 978-1-78952-329-4
Bat Out Of Hell by Meatloaf – Geoffrey Feakes 978-1-78952-320-1
Bringing It All Back Home by Bob Dylan – Opher Goodwin 978-1-78952-314-0
Crime Of The Century by Supertramp – Steve Pilkington 978-1-78952-327-0
Let It Bleed by The Rolling Stones – John Van der Kiste 978-1-78952-309-6
Purple Rain by Prince – Matt Karpe 978-1-78952-322-5

**On Screen Series**
Carry On… – Stephen Lambe 978-1-78952-004-0
David Cronenberg – Patrick Chapman 978-1-78952-071-2
Doctor Who: The David Tennant Years – Jamie Hailstone 978-1-78952-066-8
James Bond – Andrew Wild 978-1-78952-010-1
Monty Python – Steve Pilkington 978-1-78952-047-7
Seinfeld Seasons 1 to 5 – Stephen Lambe 978-1-78952-012-5

**Other Books**
1967: A Year In Psychedelic Rock 978-1-78952-155-9

1970: A Year In Rock – John Van der Kiste 978-1-78952-147-4
1972: The Year Progressive Rock Ruled The World – Kevan Furbank 978-1-78952-288-4
1973: The Golden Year of Progressive Rock 978-1-78952-165-8
Babysitting A Band On The Rocks – G.D. Praetorius 978-1-78952-106-1
Eric Clapton Sessions – Andrew Wild 978-1-78952-177-1
Dark Horse Records – Aaron Badgley 978-1-78952-287-7
Derek Taylor: For Your Radioactive Children – Andrew Darlington 978-1-78952-038-5
The Golden Age of Easy Listening – Derek Taylor 978-1-78952-285-3
The Golden Road: The Recording History of The Grateful Dead – John Kilbride 978-1-78952-156-6
Iggy and The Stooges On Stage 1967-1974 – Per Nilsen 978-1-78952-101-6
Jon Anderson and the Warriors – the road to Yes – David Watkinson 978-1-78952-059-0
Magic: The David Paton Story – David Paton 978-1-78952-266-2
Misty: The Music of Johnny Mathis – Jakob Baekgaard 978-1-78952-247-1
Nu Metal: A Definitive Guide – Matt Karpe 978-1-78952-063-7
Remembering Live Aid – Andrew Wild 978-1-78952-328-7
Tommy Bolin: In and Out of Deep Purple – Laura Shenton 978-1-78952-070-5
Maximum Darkness – Deke Leonard 978-1-78952-048-4
The Twang Dynasty – Deke Leonard 978-1-78952-049-1

*And Many More To Come!*

**Would you like to write for Sonicbond Publishing?**

We are mainly a music publisher, but we also occasionally publish in other genres including film and television. At Sonicbond Publishing we are always on the look-out for authors, particularly for our two main series, On Track and Decades.

Mixing fact with in depth analysis, the On Track series examines the entire recorded work of a particular musical artist or group. All genres are considered from easy listening and jazz to 60s soul to 90s pop, via rock and metal.

The Decades series singles out a particular decade in an artist or group's history and focuses on that decade in more detail than may be allowed in the On Track series.

While professional writing experience would, of course, be an advantage, the most important qualification is to have real enthusiasm and knowledge of your subject. First-time authors are welcomed, but the ability to write well in English is essential.

Sonicbond Publishing has distribution throughout Europe and North America, and all our books are also published in E-book form. Authors will be paid a royalty based on sales of their book.

Further details about our books are available from www.sonicbondpublishing.com. To contact us, complete the contact form there or email info@sonicbondpublishing.co.uk